mc cR

MCR

Planet Earth
Science Fair Projects

Library of Congress Cataloging-in-Publication Data
Gardner, Robert, 1929–
  Planet earth science fair projects, revised and expanded using the scientific method / Robert Gardner.
      p. cm. — (Earth science projects using the scientific method)
  Summary: "Explains how to use the scientific method to conduct several science experiments
about earth science. Includes ideas for science fair projects"—Provided by publisher.
  Includes bibliographical references and index.
  ISBN 978-0-7660-3423-5
  1. Earth science projects—Juvenile literature. 2. Science projects—Juvenile literature. I. Title.
  QE29.G376 2010
  550.78—dc22
                                        2009026546

Printed in the United States of America

102009 Lake Book Manufacturing, Inc., Melrose Park, IL

10 9 8 7 6 5 4 3 2 1

Illustration Credits: Tom LaBaff and Stephanie LaBaff

Editorial Revision: Lily Book Productions

Design: Oxygen Design

Photo Credits: Fanelli Photography/istockphoto.com, p. 26; NASA, p. 6; Shutterstock, pp. 3, 58,
84, 114, 136.

Cover Photos: © 2009 Jupiterimages Corporation (Moon); Shutterstock (Earth, hands, stars).

Revised edition of *Planet Earth Science Fair Projects Using the Moon, Stars,
Beach Balls, Frisbees, and Other Far-Out Stuff.* Copyright © 2004.

Planet Earth
Science Projects

Revised and Expanded
Using the Scientific Method

Robert Gardner

Enslow Publishers, Inc.
40 Industrial Road
Box 398
Berkeley Heights, NJ 07922
USA

http://www.enslow.com

Contents

Indicates activities appropriate for science fair projects.

INTRODUCTION

Planet Earth Experiments and Projects Using the Scientific Method

The giant sphere on which we live is our Earth. It is one of the planets in a solar system that consists of eight planets and the Sun about which they orbit.

Scientists study Earth because it is our home. It is the only planet in the solar system that can support life. From Earth, scientists can study the other planets as well. In doing so, they can measure where Earth is in relation to other cosmic entities.

In this book, you will learn where Earth is located relative to its near and distant neighbors. You will also become aware of the vast distances that separate planets from the Sun and from each other. You will discover why our only natural satellite, the Moon, changes its appearance, find ways to keep our planet healthy, and learn how to make maps of Earth's surface.

◄ Earth is the only planet known to sustain life. In this *Apollo 17* photograph, the South polar ice cap can be seen.

Experiments and Projects

This book contains lots of fun experiments about Earth. You'll also be given suggestions for independent investigations that you can do yourself. Many of the experiments are followed by a section called Science Project Ideas. This section contains great ideas for your own science fair projects.

To do some of the projects in this book, you may need people to help you, because more than one pair of hands may be required. Try to choose helpers who are patient and who enjoy experimenting as much as you do.

The experiments are all easy to do and safe to carry out when the instructions are followed as given. Consult with your school science teacher or some **other responsible adult** to obtain approval before starting any experiments of your own.

If any danger is involved in doing an experiment, it will be made known to you. In some cases, to avoid any danger to you, you'll be asked to work **with an adult**. Please do so. We don't want you to take any chances that could lead to an injury.

Most of the materials you'll need to carry out the projects and experiments described in this book can be found in your home. Several of the experiments may require items that you can buy from a supermarket, a hobby or toy shop, a hardware store, or one of the science supply companies listed in the appendix. As you begin to use this book, show it to one of the science teachers in your school. Perhaps the teacher will allow you and some of your friends to use the school's equipment.

As you do these projects, you will find it useful to record your ideas, notes, data, and anything you can conclude from your experiments in a notebook. That way you can keep track of the information you gather and the conclusions you reach. It will also allow you to refer to other experiments you've done that may be useful to you in later projects.

How Scientists
Search for Answers

When scientists have a question to answer, they start by researching. They read scientific literature and consult online science databases that are maintained by universities, research centers, or the government. There, they can study abstracts—summaries of reports—by scientists who have conducted experiments or done similar research in the field.

In this way, they find out whether other scientists have examined the same question or have tried to answer it by doing an experiment. Careful research will tell what kind of experiments, if any, have been done to try to answer the question.

Scientists don't want to repeat experiments that have known and accepted outcomes. Also, they want to avoid repeating any mistakes others may have made while doing similar experiments. If no one else has done scientific work that answers the question, scientists then do further research on how best to do the experiment.

While researching for the experiment, the scientist tries to guess—or predict—the possible results. This prediction is called a hypothesis.

The scientist hopes that a well-researched and carefully planned experiment will prove the hypothesis to be true. At times, however, the results of even the best-planned experiment can be far different from what the scientist expected. Yet even if the results indicate the hypothesis was not true, this does not mean the experiment was a failure. In fact, unexpected results can provide valuable information that leads to a different answer or to another, even better, experiment.

Using the Scientific Method in Experiments and Projects

The Scientific Method

A scientific experiment starts when someone wonders what would happen if certain conditions were set up and tested by following a specific process. In other cases, scientists must observe conditions that already exist. For example, in an experiment investigating long–term change in weather, you can ask the question: "Is there a link between hurricanes and global warming?"

A hypothesis must be a statement because it has to be proved or disproved. The hypothesis might be:

✓ Global warming has increased the frequency of hurricanes.

✓ Hurricane frequency has decreased as global warming has taken place.

✓ Hurricane frequency has remained the same.

Next, decide how you are going to do your project. In what areas are you planning to study hurricane frequency? For how long has global warming taken place, and for what periods are you planning to examine hurricanes? How reliable are these measurements?

Remember: To give your experiment or project every chance of success, prepare a hypothesis that is clear and brief. The simpler the hypothesis, the better it is.

After you have collected your data, you must examine it and decide what it means. This is the time when you will find the answers to your initial questions. You might conclude that there has been an increase in hurricane frequency for the area you studied. When you have your data and conclusions, share them with other people.

Scientists may develop logical explanations for the results of their experiments. These explanations, or theories, then must be tested by more experiments. If the resulting data from more experiments provide compelling support for a theory, then that theory could be accepted by the world of science. But scientists are careful about accepting new theories. If the resulting data contradict a theory, then the theory must be discarded, altered, or retested. That is the scientific method.

Basic Steps in the Scientific Method

The best experiments and science projects usually follow the scientific method's basic steps:

✓ Ask questions about what would happen if certain conditions or events were set up and tested in an experiment.

✓ Do background research to investigate the subject of your questions until you have a main question.

✓ Construct a hypothesis—an answer to your question—that you can then test and investigate with an experiment.

✓ Design and conduct an experiment to test your hypothesis.

✓ Keep records, collecting data, and then analyze what you've recorded.

✓ Draw a conclusion based on the experiment and the data you've recorded.

✓ Write a report about your results.

Your Hypothesis

Many experiments and science projects begin by asking how planets and other satellites behave in space. In this book's experiment, "Path of a Satellite," the question is: "Why does the path of a satellite have an S shape when seen on a flat map of the world?"

How do you search for an answer? For your hypothesis? First, you should find out how satellites are launched into space. Then you should look at a flat map and a globe for an idea of how the satellite travels.

After your research, you might make an educated guess in answer to the question; this is your hypothesis: "The path of the satellite appears S-shaped because of the way Earth is depicted on a flat surface."

You'll also find out what methods, materials, and equipment are needed to design an experiment that tests your hypothesis.

Designing the Experiment

Your experiment will be structured to investigate whether the hypothesis is true or false. The experiment is intended to test the hypothesis, not necessarily to prove that the hypothesis is right.

The results of a well-designed experiment are more valuable than the results of an experiment that is intentionally designed to give the answer you want. The conditions you set up in your experiment must be a fair test of your hypothesis. For example, in the satellite path experiment, you should get data from different satellites. These satellites should have been launched from different locations. They may also be of different sizes and be used for different activities.

Remember: Scientists around the world always use metric measurements in their experiments and projects, and so should you. Use metric liquid and dry measures and a Celsius thermometer.

By carefully carrying out your experiment you'll discover useful information that can be recorded as data. It's most important that the experiment's procedures and results are as accurate as possible. Design the experiment for observable, measurable results. And keep it simple, because the more complicated your experiment is, the more chance you have for error.

Also, if you have friends helping you with an experiment or project, make sure from the start that they'll take their tasks seriously.

Recording Data

Your hypothesis, procedure, data, and conclusions should be recorded immediately as you experiment, but don't keep this information on loose scraps of paper. Record your data in a notebook or a logbook—one you use just for experiments. Your notebook should be bound so that you have a permanent record. The laboratory notebook is an essential part of all academic and scientific research.

Make sure to include the date, experiment number, and a brief description of how you collected the data. Write clearly. If you have to cross something out, do it with just a single line, then rewrite the correct information.

Repeat your experiment several times to be sure your results are consistent and your data are trustworthy. Don't try to interpret data as you go along. It's better first to record results accurately, then study them later.

You might even find that you want to replace your experiment's original question with a new one. For example, by answering the question, "What happens to rain that falls to the ground?" you learn that water collects underground in aquifers. This brings up other questions: "What happens when an aquifer becomes very full of water? When there is little water? Can there be more than one aquifer in a location? What might cause water to move in an aquifer?"

Writing the Science Fair Report

Communicate the results of your experiment by writing a clear report. Even the most successful experiment loses its value if the scientist cannot clearly tell what happened. Your report should describe how the experiment was designed and conducted and should state its precise results.

Following are the parts of a science fair report, in the order they should appear:

• Title Page

The title of your experiment should be centered and near the top of the page. Your teacher will tell you what other information is needed, such as your name, grade, and the name of your science teacher.

• Table of Contents

On the report's second page, list the remaining parts of the report and their page numbers.

• Abstract

Give a brief overview of your experiment. In just a few sentences, tell the purpose of the experiment, what you did, and what you found out. Always write in plain, clear language.

• Introduction

State your hypothesis and explain how you came up with it. Discuss your experiment's main question and how your research led to the hypothesis. Tell what you hoped to achieve when you started the experiment.

• Experiment and Data

This is a detailed step-by-step explanation of how you organized and carried out the experiment. Explain what methods you followed and what materials and equipment you used.

State when the experiment was done (the date and perhaps the time of day) and under what conditions (in a laboratory, outside on a windy day, in cold or warm weather, etc.). Tell who was involved and what part they played in the experiment.

Include clearly labeled graphs and tables of data from the experiment as well as any photographs or drawings that help illustrate your work. Anyone who reads your report should be able to repeat the experiment just the way you did it. (Repeating an experiment is a good way to test whether the original results were obtained correctly.)

• Discussion

Explain your results and conclusions, perhaps comparing them with published scientific data you first read about in your research. Consider how the experiment's results relate to your hypothesis. Ask yourself: Do my results support or contradict my hypothesis? Then analyze the answer.

Would you do anything differently if you did this experiment again? State what you've learned as a result of the experiment.

Analyze how your tools and equipment did their tasks, and how well you and others used those tools. If you think the experiment could be done better if designed another way or if you've another hypothesis that might be tested, then include this in your discussion.

• Conclusion

Make a brief summary of your experiment's results. Include only information and data already stated in the report, and be sure not to bring in any new information.

• Acknowledgments

Give credit to everyone who helped you with the experiment. State the names of these individuals and briefly explain who they are and how they assisted you.

• References / Bibliography

List any books, magazines, journals, articles, Web sites, scientific databases, and interviews that were important to your research for the experiment.

Science Fairs

Some of the experiments in this book are followed by a section called Science Project Ideas. These ideas may be appropriate for a science fair. However, judges at science fairs do not reward projects or experiments that are simply copied from a book. For example, a model of the solar system would not impress judges. Data from personal observations of distant stars would receive far more consideration.

Science fair judges tend to reward creative thought and imagination. However, it is difficult to be creative or imaginative unless you are really interested in your project, so choose something that appeals to you. Consider, too, your own ability and the cost of materials needed for the project.

If you decide to use a project found in this book for a science fair, you will need to find ways to modify or extend it. This should not be difficult because as you do these projects you will think of new ideas for experiments. It is these new experiments that will make excellent science fair projects because they spring from your own mind and are interesting to you.

If you decide to enter a science fair and have never done so before, you should read some of the books listed in the further reading section. The references that deal specifically with science fairs will provide plenty of helpful hints and lots of useful information that will enable you to avoid the pitfalls that sometimes plague first-time entrants. You will learn how to prepare appealing reports that include charts and graphs, how to set up and display your work, how to present your project, and how to talk to judges and visitors.

Following are some suggestions to consider.

Some Tips for Success at a Science Fair

Science teachers and science fair judges have many different opinions on what makes a good science fair project or experiment. Here are the most important elements:

Originality of Concept is one of the most important things judges consider. Some judges believe that the best science fair projects answer a question that is not found in a science textbook.

Scientific Content is another main area of evaluation. How was science applied in the procedure? Are there sufficient data? Did you stick to your intended procedure and keep good records?

Thoroughness is next in importance. Was the experiment repeated as often as needed to test your hypothesis? Is your notebook complete, and are the data accurate? Does your research bibliography show you did enough library work?

Clarity in how you present your exhibit shows you had a good understanding of the subject you worked on. It's important that your exhibit clearly presents the results of your work.

Effective Process: Judges recognize that how skillfully you carry out a science fair project is usually more important than its results. A well-done project gives students the best understanding of what scientists actually do day-to-day.

Remember: Do not block your exhibit. Stand to the side when someone is looking at it.

Other points to consider when preparing for your science fair:

The Abstract: Write up a brief explanation of your project and make copies for visitors or judges who want to read it.

Knowledge: Be ready to answer questions from visitors and judges confidently. Know what is in your notebook and make some notes on index cards to remind you of important points.

Practice: Before the science fair begins, prepare a list of several questions you think you might be asked. Think about the answers and about how your display can help to support them. Have a friend or parent ask you questions and answer them out loud. Knowing your work thoroughly helps you feel more confident when you're asked about it.

Appearance: Dress and act in a way that shows you take your project seriously. Visitors and judges should get the impression that you're interested in the project and take pride in answering their questions about it.

Your observations about planet Earth will need to be displayed for the judges. Photograph the phenomena you are investigating. If you cannot take a photograph, you may be able to find photos taken by other scientists or you can draw a model. You will certainly have data from your observations. Record your data in a clear and easy to read chart or graph. Be inventive about different ways of showing what you observed.

Safety First

Most of the projects included in this book are perfectly safe, but it's your responsibility to do them only as directed. Some experiments can be dangerous unless certain precautions are taken. The precautions necessary to prevent accidents and to make the experiments safe and enjoyable are easy to follow.

✔ Do any experiments or projects, whether from this book or of your own design, under the supervision of a science teacher or **other knowledgeable adult**.

✔ If you need to use a sharp knife or a chemical, get **an adult** to help you. Do not try to manage these kinds of materials by yourself.

✔ Read all instructions carefully before proceeding with a project. If you have questions, check with your supervisor before going any further.

✔ Maintain a serious attitude while conducting experiments. Fooling around can be dangerous to you and to others.

✔ The liquid in some thermometers is mercury. It is dangerous to touch mercury or to breathe mercury vapor, and such thermometers have been banned in many states. When doing these experiments, use only non-mercury thermometers, such as those filled with alcohol. If you have a mercury thermometer in the house, **ask an adult** if it can be taken to a local mercury thermometer exchange location.

✔ Never look directly at the Sun. It can permanently damage your eyes.

✔ Wear approved safety goggles when you are working with a flame or doing anything that might cause injury to your eyes.

✔ Do not put your fingers or any object other than properly designed electrical connectors into electrical outlets.

✔ Never experiment with household electricity except under the supervision of a **knowledgeable adult**.

✔ Do not eat or drink during an experiment.

And now, on to the experiments!

MOON

EARTH

CHAPTER 1

Where Are We?
Earth in Space

Earth has a diameter of 12,756 kilometers (7,926 mi) and a circumference, at its equator, of 40,073 kilometers (24,900 mi). Every day, at most places on Earth, we see a nearby star rise above the horizon, move slowly across the blue dome we call sky, and sink below the opposite horizon. We named the star Sun, and the time between one sunrise and the next is called a day.

The direction toward the horizon where the Sun rises is called east. The direction toward the horizon where the Sun sets is termed west. After the Sun sinks below the western horizon far enough that even the sunlight reflected by the air disappears, we are left in darkness. But the darkness is not total. Lacking the Sun's bright light, we can see the dim light from many, many more distant stars. On some nights, Earth is illuminated by light from an object brighter than the stars. It appears to be about the size of the Sun, although much less brilliant. It is the Moon. Its shape seems to slowly change night by night from a mere bent sliver to a full circle and back to a sliver before it disappears, only to return again as a sliver. Like the Sun, the stars and the Moon in the night sky appear to move from east to west.

◀ In our solar system, Earth orbits the Sun, and the Moon orbits Earth.

The distant stars seem to be in fixed places relative to one another. However, there are points of light that move slowly across the distant stars. Early stargazers called these points of light *planets*, from a Greek word meaning "wanderer." Later, after examining them through telescopes, astronomers determined that the planets were not stars. Like Earth, they are spheres that reflect the Sun's light but emit none of their own.

Seventy percent of Earth is covered with water, mostly deep oceans of salty water. Earth's dry land, which makes up only 30 percent of its surface, is divided into seven continents—North America, South America, Europe, Asia, Africa, Australia, and Antarctica. Some geographers regard Europe and Asia as a single continent, which they call Eurasia.

Earth's crust, on which we stand, is about 19 to 64 kilometers (12 to 40 mi) thick beneath continents, and 5 to 11 kilometers (3 to 6.7 mi) thick beneath the oceans. It is made up mostly of lightweight rocks (see Figure 1a).

The mantle, which lies below Earth's crust, consists primarily of silica and minerals rich in iron, magnesium, and other metals. It is about 2,900 kilometers (1,800 mi) thick and makes up 84 percent of Earth's volume and 67 percent of its weight.

Earth's core, which lies between Earth's center and its mantle, has two parts. The outer core is about 2,250 kilometers (1,400 mi) thick. The inner core, extending outward from Earth's center, is about 1,290 kilometers (800 mi) thick. The inner core is believed to be mostly solid iron together with some other dense elements, such as nickel. The same materials make up the outer core, which seems to be liquid.

Figure 1.

a)

b)

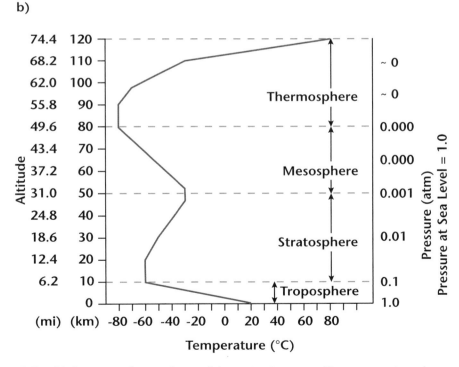

a) Earth's layers are known by studying seismic waves. These waves travel beneath Earth's surface at speeds that depend on the density of the matter through which they move.

b) The diagram shows how temperature and air pressure change throughout Earth's atmosphere.

Above the planet's surface lies an atmosphere of air that contains enough oxygen, which makes life possible. We live at the bottom of that ocean of air, most of which is within 100 kilometers (62 mi) of Earth's crust, as shown in Figure 1b. The troposphere, the first 11 kilometers (7 mi) of air above the surface, is where we live and where weather takes place. As we ascend into the troposphere, air temperature and pressure decrease. However, in the stratosphere, the temperature of the very thin air rises, only to fall again in the mesosphere. The stratosphere has a layer of ozone that absorbs much of the Sun's dangerous ultraviolet radiation. Temperatures decline through the mesosphere, then rise again in the thermosphere.

Not shown in the diagram is the ionosphere, which extends from 48 to 400 kilometers (30 to 250 mi) above Earth's surface. In the ionosphere, air molecules are ionized (changed to charged particles) by the Sun's radiation. The ionosphere reflects radio waves, making radio communication possible over long distances. Unaware that the ionosphere existed, Thomas Edison predicted that Guglielmo Marconi's attempt to send radio waves across the ocean from North America to England would fail. He believed that Earth's curvature would cause radio waves to move along a straight path into outer space. Marconi had evidence that radio waves were reflected by something in the atmosphere. Much to Edison's astonishment, Marconi was successful in establishing long-range communication using electromagnetic waves.

EXPERIMENT 1.1

Air Pressure, Temperature, and Altitude

Question:

How does air pressure and temperature change as you ascend a mountain?

Hypothesis:

As you ascend in the troposphere, both air temperature and air pressure decrease.

Materials:

- **an adult**
- outdoor thermometer
- notebook and pencil
- aneroid barometer
- mountain

Pressure is defined as force per area. When you stand on a floor, your entire weight (a force) pushes on an area equal to the area of your feet. If you weigh 50 kilograms (110 lb) and the area of your shoes is 400 square centimeters (62 in²), the pressure you exert on the floor is

$$\frac{50 \text{ kg}}{400 \text{ cm}^2} = 0.125 \text{ kg/cm}^2 \quad \text{or} \quad \frac{110 \text{ lb}}{62 \text{ in}^2} = 1.77 \text{ lb/in}^2$$

Procedure:

1. Use a thermometer to measure air temperature at the base of a mountain. Record that temperature. At the same time, use an aneroid barometer to measure air pressure at the base of the mountain.

   An aneroid barometer (Figure 2a) has a hole in the back where air can enter. The air pushes against a sealed, thin, hollow metal can from which most of the air has been removed. The outside of the can is attached to a spring. A series of levers connects the spring to a chain that turns a pointer over the barometer's dial, shown in Figure 2b. Often there will be a needle that can be set by hand so that you can see whether the pressure is increasing or decreasing over time.

   When air pressure increases, the sides of the can are pushed inward, stretching the spring. The spring pulls on the chain, turning the pointer toward a larger number on the dial. When air pressure decreases, the sides of the can move outward and the spring is under less tension. The pointer moves back to a smaller number on the dial.

2. **With an adult**, travel to the top of the mountain and again measure and record the air temperature and pressure. Do your results confirm your prediction? How might differences in time of day at the base and top of the mountain affect your measurements?

   If there are no mountains nearby, you could carry the barometer from the basement of a tall building to the top of the same building. How many floors do you have to ascend before you can detect a change in air pressure?

   If you live in a multistory house or apartment, can you detect a change in pressure between the bottom and top floors of the house or apartment?

3. What is the altitude at the top and base of the mountain? Estimate the change in pressure and temperature per meter (or foot) of altitude.

a)

Figure 2.

a) A side-view diagram of an aneroid barometer.

b) The dial of an aneroid barometer, which allows you to measure air pressure. Most aneroid barometers show pressure in inches of mercury. Normal atmospheric pressure at sea level is 30 inches of mercury, which is the same as 14.7 pounds per square inch or 1.04 kilograms per square centimeter.

b)

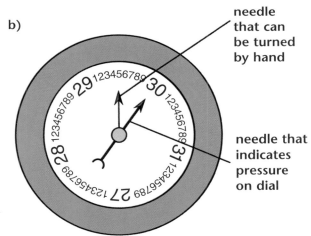

Results and Conclusions

Since we live at the bottom of an ocean of air, there is a long column of air above us. Like you, that tall column of air has weight. The air's weight pushes against you and everything else, just as your weight pushes on a floor when you stand on it. This air pressure changes at different points in Earth's atmosphere. Were you able to detect any changes?

Science Project Ideas

- Do some research on Blaise Pascal (1623–1662), a French mathematician and physicist. What experiment did Pascal perform at the Puy de Dôme in France in 1648? What led him to perform this experiment? Can you duplicate it using an aneroid barometer?

- Who was Evangelista Torricelli (1608–1647) and what did he invent? For what discovery is he famous? Can you duplicate his experiment using water?

- As you ascend a mountain or take off in an airplane, do you often sense a strange feeling in your ears? Can that feeling be eliminated by swallowing or moving your jaw? How can you explain the strange feeling? How might swallowing or moving your jaw return your ears to normal?

EXPERIMENT 1.2

Pressure, Temperature, and Depth

Question:

How do pressure and temperature change in deep water?

Hypothesis:

Pressure increases in deep water, but temperature decreases.

Materials:

- **an adult**
- aneroid barometer
- clear plastic bag
- pail
- water, cold and warm
- deep lake or pond
- boat and life vests
- thermometer (-10°C–110°C)
- watch
- weight, such as a lead sinker
- long piece of fishing line
- string
- eyedropper
- food coloring
- 2 clear plastic vials or small drinking glasses

Procedure:

1. To see how pressure changes with the depth of the water, place an aneroid barometer in a clear plastic bag. Seal the bag so that water cannot enter it. Then lower the enclosed barometer into a pail of water. What happens to the pressure inside the bag as you lower it deeper into the water? How can you explain the change in pressure?

2. To see the effect of water depth on temperature, you will need some deep water, such as a lake or a pond. **Accompanied by an adult and wearing life vests**, take a boat to the center of a deep lake or pond. Use a thermometer to measure the temperature of the water at the pond's surface.

3. Tie a weight to the end of a long piece of fishing line. Tie the thermometer to the weight or line. Lower the line into the water so that the thermometer is carried deep down into the pond. After five minutes, quickly raise the thermometer and read the thermometer. How does the depth of the water affect its temperature?

4. To see why the temperature changes with depth, you will need an eyedropper, food coloring, two clear plastic vials or small drinking glasses, and warm and cold water. Place a drop of food coloring in one vial or glass. Nearly fill that vial with cold water. Add a similar amount of warm water to the second vial or glass.

5. Next, use the eyedropper to remove some of the cold colored water. Place the end of the eyedropper just below the surface of the warm water, as shown in Figure 3. Slowly squeeze the bulb of the eyedropper so that a small amount of cold colored water enters the warm water. What happens to the cold water? Does it rise, sink, or stay where you put it?

Results and Conclusions

Not only are there pressure changes as you ascend or descend in the atmosphere, but there are also pressure differences at different depths of

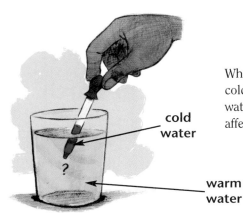

Figure 3.

What happens when a drop of cold water is placed in warm water? Is the density of water affected by temperature?

cold water

warm water

water. When you dive into a swimming pool, you can probably feel a change in pressure in your ears.

What do your experiments tell you about the density (weight per volume) of cold water, as compared with warm water? How does this experiment help explain why the temperature of water is related to its depth in a lake or a pond?

 Science Project Ideas

- If cold water is denser than warm water, why does ice float? Is there some temperature at which the density of colder water becomes less than that of warmer water? If so, what is that temperature? Can you offer experimental evidence for such a temperature?

- How does the pressure at the deepest point in the Pacific Ocean (11,033 meters, or 36,198 feet) compare with the pressure of the atmosphere at Earth's surface?

- There is no air on the Moon, so the Moon's surface is in a very good vacuum. How did the astronauts who walked on the Moon manage to survive in such a vacuum?

EXPERIMENT 1.3

Evidence for a Spherical Earth

Question:
Is a sphere the only object that will *always* cast a round shadow?

Hypothesis:
Only a sphere will always cast a round shadow.

Materials:
- lamp with lightbulb
- dark room
- sphere, such as
  a soccer ball
  or a beach ball
- Frisbee or jar lid
- cylinder, such as an
  aluminum can
- cone-shaped object

Procedure:

1. Place a single lightbulb near one side of an otherwise dark room. The bulb will be used to cast shadows of objects held near a wall on the opposite side of the room.

2. Begin with a sphere, such as a soccer ball or a beach ball. Hold the sphere near the wall and turn it in various ways. Does the sphere always cast a round shadow?

3. Are there other shapes that will always cast round shadows? To find out, test for a disk-shaped Earth using a Frisbee or a jar lid. Can you hold the disk so that it casts a round shadow? Can the disk cast shadows that are not round? If so, how many different shadow shapes can it cast?

4. Use a cylinder, such as an aluminum can, to cast shadows. Can a cylinder cast a round shadow? Can it cast shadows with other shapes? If so, how many differently shaped shadows can it cast?

5. How about a cone? Can it cast a round shadow? Can it cast shadows with other shapes? If so, how many different shadow shapes can it cast? What other objects might cast round shadows? Do these objects *always* cast a round shadow?

6. Perhaps you have noticed that on a clear day, if you look across the sea to the horizon, an incoming ship's mast and sails will be seen before its hull. Do you see how a spherical Earth can explain why the taller parts of a ship appear first as it sails toward you?

Results and Conclusions

Ancient sailors often avoided sailing beyond sight of land. They feared they would fall off the edge of what they believed was a disk-shaped Earth. You have probably seen photographs of Earth taken from space or from the Moon's surface. Such photographs provide convincing evidence that Earth is a sphere. But these photographs did not surprise anyone. People have known for centuries that we live on a sphere. Although ancient sailors believed that Earth was flat, astronomers and geographers of the same era knew Earth was round. How did they know?

Aristotle (384–322 B.C.), a famous Greek philosopher, offered evidence of Earth's spherical shape. He noticed that during an eclipse of the Moon, the edge of Earth's shadow could be seen on the lunar surface. That shadow was always curved. Aristotle argued that only a sphere can cast a shadow that is always round. Is this true?

Aristotle also noted that sailors on ships sailing northward would observe previously unseen stars appear on the northern horizon, while stars on the southern horizon disappeared. The opposite was true when they sailed southward. As Figure 4 demonstrates, this effect could easily be explained by a spherical Earth.

Figure 4.

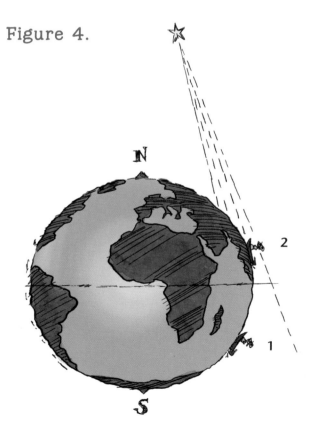

At position 1 on a spherical Earth, the light from a certain star cannot be seen. By moving north to position 2, the star becomes visible. Its light is no longer blocked by Earth.

Earth's Imaginary Grid and a Canopy of Stars

Positions on Earth are established from a giant imaginary grid that covers the planet's surface (see Figure 5). These are the lines you see on a world map or a globe. The lines that run from the North Pole to the South Pole are called meridians. These lines measure longitude. The prime meridian is zero degrees longitude. It passes through Greenwich, England. If you look on a globe, you will see that the distance between these longitude lines is greatest

Figure 5.

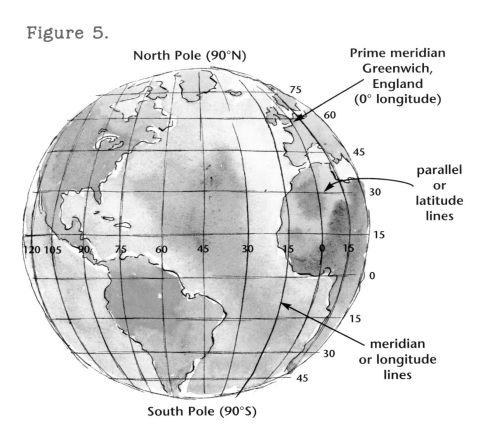

North Pole (90°N)

Prime meridian
Greenwich,
England
(0° longitude)

parallel
or
latitude
lines

meridian
or longitude
lines

South Pole (90°S)

We use an imaginary grid over Earth to pinpoint locations. Meridians, lines of longitude, give us our east-west position. Parallels, lines of latitude, give us our north-south position. Philadelphia is approximately 75° west of Greenwich England, which is 0° longitude, and 40° north of the equator, which is 0° latitude. Can you find it on a globe?

at the equator. The lines join to form a point at each pole. Because there are 360 degrees in a circle and 24 hours in one day (one revolution of Earth), the major meridian lines are 15 degrees apart (360° ÷ 24 hr = 15°/hr). This is also why time zones are about 15 degrees apart. For political and economic reasons, time zones in many countries are not exactly 15 degrees apart.

When you move westward from one time zone to the next, you set your clock back one hour.

Imaginary lines parallel to the equator are called parallels. They are used to measure latitude—degrees north or south of the equator. Degrees of latitude are about 111 kilometers (69 mi) apart. The North Pole is 90 degrees latitude. The equator is 0 degrees latitude. How far is it from the North Pole to the equator?

When you look up at the night sky, you see hundreds of stars spread out over what looks to be a slightly flattened dome. This canopy of stars is known as the celestial sphere. We can use the stars in the celestial sphere to determine our position on Earth. You will see how we do that in Experiment 1.5. But first, you need to know something about the light that comes from stars.

EXPERIMENT 1.4

The Light from Stars

Question:

How does light from stars travel to Earth?

Hypothesis:

All light travels in straight lines.

Materials:

- clear lightbulb with line filament
- socket for bulb
- straight pins
- sheet of cardboard
- dark room
- sunlight
- ruler

Procedure:

1. A clear lightbulb with a line filament can be used to represent a star (Figure 6). The bulb is placed in a socket and turned so that the end of the filament is facing you. The end of the filament is just a point of light. The same is true of a distant star. It is just a small dot set in the dark sky.

2. Stick three straight pins side by side and about one centimeter (0.4 in) apart at one end of a sheet of cardboard. In a dark room, hold the pins close to the point of light. You will see that the shadows of the pins diverge (spread apart). But what happens as you move the pins farther from the light?

side view of lightbulb

end of filament

pins

shadows of pins

Figure 6.

The end of a line filament looks like a point of light. It can be used to represent light from a star. Shadows of pins can be used to show that light rays reaching Earth from a distant star are parallel.

Results and Conclusions

As you have just seen, light rays from a source of light that is far away are parallel (or very nearly so) and, therefore, the pins cast parallel shadows. What do you think will happen if these three pins are placed in sunlight? Do you think their shadows will be parallel?

 Science Project Ideas

- What is the definition of *parallax*? Design an experiment to demonstrate parallax. How is parallax used to measure the distance to stars?

- Design and carry out an experiment to estimate the number of all the stars that are visible in the night sky.

EXPERIMENT 1.5

Using a Star to Find Your Latitude

Question:

What is the latitude of where you live?

Hypothesis:

You can find your latitude by measuring the altitude of the North Star (Polaris), which is located almost directly above Earth's North Pole.

Materials:

- clear night
- astrolabe
- helper
- chalk or other object for drawing line on ground

As you can see from Figure 7, the altitude of Polaris (its angle of elevation above the horizon) is equal to the latitude from which its altitude is measured. At the North Pole, latitude 90 degrees, it is directly overhead, an altitude of 90 degrees. At the equator, latitude 0 degrees, it is on the horizon, an altitude of 0 degrees. At a latitude of 45 degrees, the altitude of Polaris is 45 degrees.

Figure 7.

You can find your latitude. It is equal to the altitude of the North Star (Polaris). Horizons in the diagram are shown as lines that are parallel to Earth's surface.

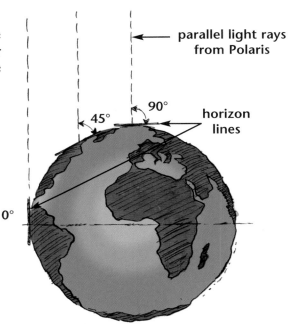

Procedure:

1. To find Polaris, go outside on a clear night. Look to the northern half of the sky to find the Big Dipper. It consists of a group of bright stars that look like the side of a cooking pan, as shown in Figure 8a. Depending on the season and the time of night, the Big Dipper may be turned at different angles in the sky. The pointer stars, Dubhe and Merak, form a line that always points toward Polaris. The distance from Polaris to the Big Dipper is about five times the distance between these two pointer stars. Do not expect to find a very bright star. Polaris, the star at the end of the handle of the Little Dipper, is about as bright as Merak.

2. To measure the altitude of Polaris, build an astrolabe like the one shown in Figure 8b.

Figure 8.

a)

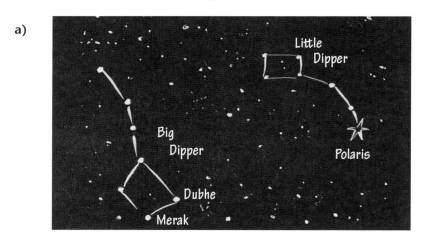

a) The Big Dipper stars Merak and Dubhe form a line that points to Polaris. Five times the distance between these two stars is approximately the distance from Dubhe to Polaris.

b)

b) An astrolabe can be made from cardboard, string, a straw, tape, a weight, and a protractor. Sight on a star through the straw. The string will mark the altitude of the star in degrees.

3. When you look at the North Star through the soda straw, the string will hang along a line that measures the star's altitude. Have a partner read the astrolabe when you have located Polaris in your straw. What is the altitude of Polaris? What is the latitude of your location?

4. While you are measuring the North Star's altitude, have someone help you mark a north-south line of sight along level ground. To do this, stand looking at Polaris. Direct your helper to move until he or she is directly under your sight line to Polaris. A straight line drawn from you to your helper will provide a north-south line that will be useful in the next experiment.

Results and Conclusions

Because Polaris is so far from Earth, light rays coming from the star are parallel, as you found they would be in the previous experiment. Any light rays that were not parallel would not hit Earth. Because of its position above the North Pole, Polaris can be used to measure latitude. Were you able to measure your latitude? How accurate was your measurement? Check a map that marks latitude to verify your measurement.

 Science Project Ideas

- Use your astrolabe to find the angle between Polaris and Dubhe. What is the angle between Merak and Dubhe?

- If Merak and Dubhe were both ten light-years away from Earth (they aren't), what would be the distance between them in light-years and in kilometers?

EXPERIMENT 1.6

Finding Your Longitude

Question:
What is the longitude of where you live?

Hypothesis:
You can find your longitude by finding the time of midday.

Materials:
- accurate clock or watch
- north-south line drawn in previous experiment
- stick
- GPS (Global Positing System) receiver (optional)

Finding your longitude is not as easy as finding your latitude. With an accurate timepiece and knowledge of the time in Greenwich, England, you can determine your approximate longitude by measuring the time of midday.

Procedure:

1. You can establish midday using the north-south line you drew in the previous experiment. Place a stick vertically at the south end of your north-south line. When the stick's shadow falls on the north-south line, you know that the Sun is midway across the sky and, therefore, it is midday.

   Midday will probably not occur at noon. For the average time zone, it takes an hour for the Sun to move from the zone's eastern edge to its western edge. Furthermore, the time of midday for any location varies with the season.

2. Suppose, for example, that you find midday occurs at 12:35 P.M. If you know it is 7:00 P.M. in Greenwich, the time difference since it was midday in Greenwich is 6 hours and 25 minutes. Since every hour represents a change of 15 degrees, you know you are 96.25 degrees west of Greenwich.

$$6 \text{ hours and } 25 \text{ minutes} = 6\,\tfrac{25}{60} \text{ hours} = 6.417 \text{ hours}$$

$$6.417 \text{ hr} \times 15°/\text{hr} = 96.25°$$

   Your longitude is 96.25° west of Greenwich, somewhere in the midwestern United States.

3. Use your north-south line and a clock or a watch to estimate your longitude. How closely does it agree with a value you can find on a map or a globe?

Results and Conclusions

Sailors used to use a sextant to take five or more sightings of the Sun beginning about 20 minutes prior to midday and another five during the 20 minutes after midday. These readings were used to determine the exact time of midday.

Today, hikers, canoeists, and others traveling through wilderness can find their position very accurately using a GPS (Global Positioning System) receiver. These relatively inexpensive handheld receivers can pick up signals from satellites orbiting Earth.

The GPS uses 24 NAVSTAR satellites orbiting Earth's poles at altitudes of more than 16,000 kilometers (10,000 mi). The satellites contain atomic clocks that transmit radio signals at very precise times. Receivers equipped with computers compare the times the signals were sent with the time they were received. With this information, the distance of the receiver from the satellites can be established, since radio signals travel at the speed of light (300,000 km/s, or 186,000 mi/s).

Because times can be measured to tenths of microseconds (0.0000001 s) or better, your position can be found to within a few meters of your true location. Your longitude and latitude are displayed on a screen.

If possible, use a GPS receiver to find your latitude and longitude. How closely do they agree with the values you found in your experiments?

 ## Science Project Ideas

- **What is the loran system of navigation and how does it work?**

- **How many signals need to be received from different satellites for a GPS receiver to determine your longitude and latitude?**

EXPERIMENT 1.7

Does Earth Turn?

Question:

How can you tell that Earth turns?

Hypothesis:

A Foucault pendulum shows that Earth rotates.

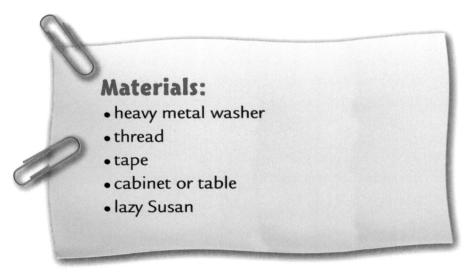

Materials:

- heavy metal washer
- thread
- tape
- cabinet or table
- lazy Susan

The Sun's position in the sky changes at a rate of 15 degrees per hour. The Sun only appears to move. It is really Earth rotating from west to east that makes the Sun appear to move from east to west. Since the time of Galileo (1564–1642), astronomers were quite certain that even though the Sun, Moon, and stars appear to move around Earth, it is really Earth that turns. But how could they be certain?

There was no direct proof that the Earth moved, rather than the Sun, Moon, and stars, until 1851 when Jean Foucault (1819–1868), a French physicist, carried out an experiment to show that Earth really does rotate.

Foucault hung a 65-meter-(213-ft-)long pendulum with a 28-kilogram (62-lb) bob from the dome of the Pantheon in Paris. Foucault knew that a pendulum will maintain the plane of its swing. He reasoned that if Earth really turns, the plane of the pendulum's swing should appear to move westward as Earth rotated beneath it.

Procedure:

1. You can make a simple model to show how a Foucault pendulum works. Make a pendulum from a heavy metal washer and a piece of thread. Use tape to hang the pendulum from a cabinet or a table, as shown in Figure 9.

2. Set the pendulum swinging above a lazy Susan. The center of the lazy Susan represents Earth's North Pole. Use a piece of tape to show the plane of the pendulum's swing.

3. Slowly turn the lazy Susan from west to east (counterclockwise) to represent a rotating Earth.

Results and Conclusions

Notice how the plane of the pendulum's swing appears to rotate from east to west just as Foucault's pendulum did in the Pantheon. What does this tell you about Earth's movement?

Some science museums and colleges have Foucault pendulums. If you go to such a place, you can see for yourself that Earth truly does rotate.

Figure 9.

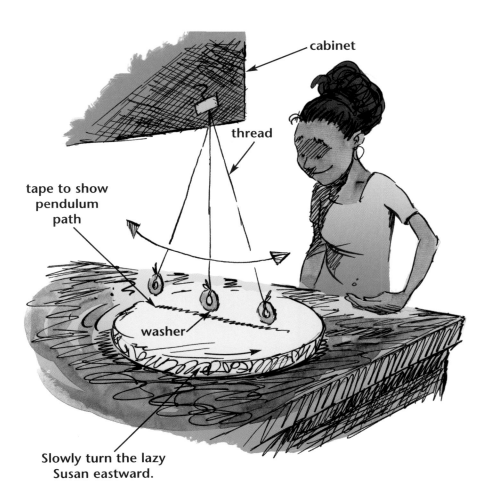

cabinet

thread

tape to show
pendulum
path

washer

Slowly turn the lazy
Susan eastward.

In the model, the center of the lazy Susan represents Earth's North Pole. What
happens to the apparent path of the pendulum as "Earth" turns from west to east?

EXPERIMENT 1.8

Path of a Satellite

Question:

Why does the path of a satellite have an S shape when seen on a flat map of the world?

Hypothesis:

The path of the satellite appears S-shaped because of the way Earth is depicted on a flat surface.

Materials:

- globe
- string
- flat projection map of the world
- pencil
- partner

Procedure:

1. Find a map (on television or in a newspaper) showing the path of a satellite (See Figure 10).

2. Obtain a globe, a piece of string long enough to go around the globe at its equator, a flat map of the world, a pencil, and a partner. The string can be used to show the satellite's path around the globe. Begin by assuming the satellite is launched from Cape Kennedy in Florida. The string then should pass over Cape Kennedy and be so oriented that half the orbit is above the equator and half below.

3. Have a partner hold the string in place firmly against the globe. On the globe, note the maximum distance of the string (orbit) above the equator.

4. Use a pencil to mark that point on the flat map of the world. Do the same for the maximum distance below the equator. Then make an X at Cape Kennedy on the flat map of the world. Continue to note familiar points through which the string passes and transfer those points to the flat map. You will need to mark about 15 to 20 such points on the map.

5. Once the marks have been made on the map, connect them with a smooth curved line.

Figure 10.

The dotted line shows the path of a satellite projected on a flat map of the world.

Results and Conclusions

On a flat map, satellites appear to follow an S-shaped path, rather than a circular or elliptical one. In this experiment, you transferred the path to a spherical globe. What does the satellite's path look like on the globe?

CHAPTER 2

The Moon: Our Largest and Only Natural Satellite

Objects that move around (orbit) a planet are called satellites. There are many satellites orbiting Earth. All but one of them have been placed in orbit by humans. Rockets launched some of them into space from Earth; space shuttles already in orbit released others. Earth's only natural satellite is the Moon. Some planets, such as Jupiter, have many moons. Earth has only one.

In this chapter, you will investigate the Moon by watching it and seeing how it changes with time. You may be surprised to learn that you can often see the Moon during the day as well as at night. There are also days when you can't see it at any time. You will track the Moon's path about Earth and the Sun. And you will make models to demonstrate what happens when Earth passes between the Moon and the Sun, or the Moon between Earth and the Sun.

◀The Moon is Earth's only natural satellite. Its appearance changes because the Sun shines on different parts of the Moon during the month.

EXPERIMENT 2.1

Watching the Moon by Day and by Night

Question:

Does the Moon's appearance change?

Hypothesis:

Over the course of one month, the Moon's appearance and location in the sky can be studied.

Materials:

- daily newspaper with information about the Moon
- notebook and pencil

Procedure:

1. To see how the Moon changes over time, you will need to record your observations about the Moon in a notebook. A good time to begin your observations is one or two days after a new moon. When the Moon is between Earth and the Sun, it is called a new moon. A newspaper or an almanac will give the date of a new moon. You can usually find this information in the weather section of the paper. Several days after the date of a new moon, look for the Moon as the Sun sets.

   You can look at the Moon as much as you want. **But never look directly at the Sun. It can cause serious damage to your eyes!**

2. Each time you observe the Moon, use a notebook to record the date, the time, and a drawing to show what the Moon looks like. You should also record the direction in which you find the Moon—north (N), south (S), east (E), west (W), or a direction in between, such as southwest (SW). Record, too, the altitude of the Moon above the horizon and, if possible, the distance (angle) between the Moon and the Sun.

Distances and altitudes in the sky are usually measured as angles. Sometimes the Sun and the Moon appear close together in the sky. They might be less than 20 degrees apart because they lie near the same imaginary line extending from your eye into space.

The Sun and the Moon are actually about 150 million kilometers (93 million mi) apart. Since the Moon orbits Earth, its average distance from the Sun is the same as Earth's distance from the Sun. When people say the Moon is close to the Sun, they mean that the angle between the Moon and the Sun in the sky is small (see Figure 11a).

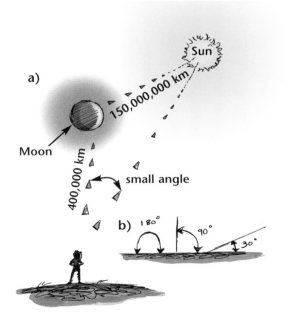

Figure 11.

a) Even though the Sun and the Moon are far apart, they may appear to be close together in the sky.
b) These are some of the angles between the Sun and the Moon that you may measure.

3. You can make good estimates of angles by using your fists. If you hold your fist at arm's length as shown in Figure 12a, it will cover approximately 10 degrees in the sky. To see that each fist really is equal to about 10 degrees, start with your fist closed and extended toward the horizon (azimuth). Go fist on fist upward, as shown in the drawing, until one arm points straight up. You will find it takes just about 9 fists to reach this point. Since horizontal to straight overhead (the zenith) is 90 degrees, each fist must cover about 10 degrees ($90° \div 9 = 10°$).

4. To find the angular distance between the Sun and the Moon, cover the Sun with one of your hands as you begin so that **you are not looking directly at the Sun**. Then find how many fists separate the Sun and the Moon. Record the angle between the Sun and the Moon in your notebook. A typical record for one observation in this experiment is shown in Figure 12b.

5. On each clear evening for the next few days, try to observe the Moon at about the time of sunset. Make the same measurements you made before and record them in your notebook. Also look for the Moon early in the morning, before sunrise, and at other times of the day and night. Record all your observations of the Moon in your notebook.

Results and Conclusions

You should already be observing some changes in the Moon. What happens to the shape of the Moon as days pass? What happens to the distance (angle) between the Moon and the Sun from one sunset to the next? What happens to the Moon's location in the sky at sunset as the days pass? Is the Moon moving more to the east or to the west of the Sun as days go by? What does this tell you about the time that the Moon rises? Is it rising earlier or later each day?

a)

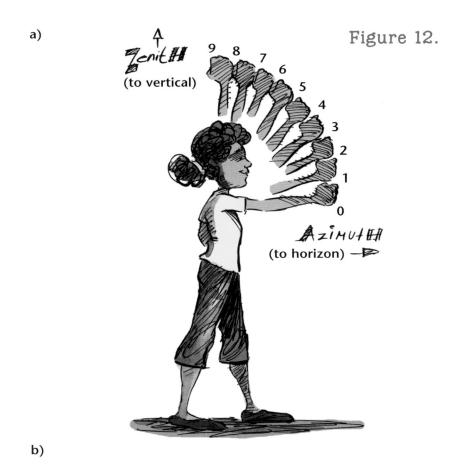

Figure 12.

b)

Moon Data				
Appearance	**Direction**	**Date & Time**	**Altitude**	**Sun-Moon Angle**
☽	SW	11/4, 4:10 P.M.	30°	25°

a) Hold your fist at arm's length, the top of your fist even with the horizon. Then go upward fist on fist until one fist is directly over your head. You will find you have gone 9 fists to cover the 90 degrees from horizontal to overhead. This means your fist at arm's length covers about 10 degrees of sky.

b) Sample data for one observation of the Moon.

Procedure:

1. About two weeks after a new moon, if it is clear, you will see a full moon. Where is the Sun when you see a full moon rising? Record your observations.

2. Keep recording data about the Moon as far into the evening as possible. Can you see the Moon the next morning when you get up?

3. When the Moon is no longer visible at sunset, begin looking for it early in the morning, before, during, and after sunrise.

Results and Conclusions

What kinds of changes do you observe? Through approximately how many degrees does the Moon move in one hour? How could you estimate the distance (angle) between the Sun and Moon even if the Sun has set?

What is the Moon's shape? Which side of the Moon (left or right) is now the brighter side? Is this the side nearer or farther from the Sun?

You may choose to continue your observations of the Moon for several months. You will begin to see a pattern to the Moon's motion and changing appearance. How much time passes between one full moon and the next? Does the full moon always rise in the same place (direction) on the horizon?

 Science Project Ideas

- Jupiter, the largest planet in our solar system, has many moons. You can see some of them by looking through binoculars. How many can you see? How can you tell that they go around the planet?

- Do some research to find out how many moons orbit each of the planets in our solar system. Are there any planets that have no satellites?

EXPERIMENT 2.2

A Model of Moon, Earth, and Sun

Question:

How do the Moon, Earth, and Sun move in relation to one another?

Hypothesis:

A model can be used to show the movement of the Moon and Earth in relation to the Sun.

Materials:

- dark room
- lamp and lightbulb
- partner
- light-colored ball, about 5 to 10 centimeters (2 to 4 in) in diameter (such as a Styrofoam ball), mounted on a stick or a nail

Scientists often make models (theories) to explain what they observe and the data they collect. In some cases the theory can be illustrated by a physical model. In this experiment, you will examine a physical model of the Moon, Earth, and Sun to see if it agrees with the data you collected in the previous experiment.

Procedure:

1. Put a single bright lightbulb at one end of a dark room. The lightbulb represents the Sun. Ask a partner to stand beside you and hold a light-colored ball mounted on a stick. If the ball is made of Styrofoam, the stick can be pushed into the ball. If you can't find a Styrofoam ball, use a tennis ball mounted on a long nail. Have your partner stand to your left while you face the light, as shown in Figure 13.

In this model, your head represents Earth; the light-colored ball is the Moon. Since you are facing the Sun (the light in this model), the model now represents Earth at noon when the Sun is in the middle of its path across the sky. The Moon (small ball) is to the east.

Figure 13.

This model represents Earth, Moon, and Sun.

2. Slowly turn your head and body toward the east (toward the Moon). Your turning represents Earth as it rotates on its axis. In your model, you are seeing the Moon rise. After you make one quarter of a turn, the Sun (lightbulb) will be on your right (west). It is sunset. The Moon is directly in front of you, so it is in the middle of the sky.

   Figure 14a shows Earth (your head), Moon (ball), and Sun (lightbulb) in your model from above. You (Earth) are facing the Moon after a one-quarter turn. Half the Moon is lighted, the other half is dark. The Moon is at first quarter. Have you ever seen the Moon when it looked like this? If you have, at what angle was it from the Sun?

3. Continue to turn slowly to your left to represent a rotating Earth. You will see the Moon set after another one-quarter turn. As you continue to rotate, you will see the Sun rise and move slowly across the "sky." Then you will again face the Moon.

4. Next, have your partner slowly move the Moon (ball) one quarter of the way around you while you make seven complete rotations (turns). Watch what happens to the Moon's appearance as you make these turns. When you face the Moon now (Figure 14b), it will be a full moon. (If the Moon is in the shadow of your head, have your partner raise the ball.)

5. During another seven turns of Earth, the Moon will move slowly to the position shown in Figure 14c. At this point, again only half the Moon you see is bright (last quarter). But it is now the other half that receives the "sunshine." After another seven turns of Earth, the Moon will lie between Earth and the Sun (Figure 14d). Since no reflected light can reach you, you will not see the Moon. It is a new moon.

Of course, a room is not a perfect model of space. Some light reflected by the walls and ceiling will reach the ball. This makes the dimly lighted ball visible. In the space around the real Moon, there are no walls or ceilings to reflect light, so it cannot be seen. The lighted side faces the Sun.

Figure 14.

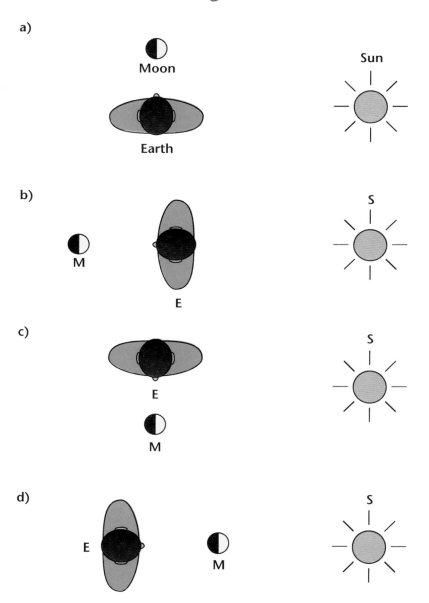

The model can be used to show the position of the Moon at (a) first quarter; (b) full moon; (c) third quarter; (d) new moon.

6. Repeat the experiment once more. While you (Earth) turn about 28 times, have your partner move the Moon once around you. Then give your partner a chance to be the rotating Earth while you move the Moon.

Results and Conclusions

A good model will agree with what is found in the real world. Does the model you have just examined agree with the observations of the Moon that you made in Experiment 2.1?

Did the real Moon change from a thin crescent to a half moon, then to a full moon? Did it then, after a week, appear as another half moon (with the opposite side bright)? Over the following week did it again become a crescent (but reversed), and then disappear before returning as a thin crescent near sunset?

If your answers to these questions are all yes, then your model of the Moon is a good one. According to the model, as Earth rotates on its axis, the Moon moves around Earth every 28 days (about once a month).

What is a "blue moon?" What is meant by the phrase "once in a blue moon?"

 Science Project Ideas

- Although lunar satellites have photographed all sides of the Moon, only astronauts have actually seen the far side of the Moon. Design a model to show why we always see the same side of the Moon.

- You have seen a crescent moon shortly after sunset. What does that same crescent moon look like to someone in Argentina? Design a model to explain.

EXPERIMENT 2.3

The Moon's Orbit About Earth and Sun

Question:

What is the shape of the Moon's orbit around the Sun?

Hypothesis:

As the Moon orbits Earth, it weaves in and out of Earth's solar orbit.

Materials:
- tape
- wrapping paper
- meterstick
- string
- friend
- pencil or marking pen
- protractor
- scissors

According to the model you examined in the previous experiment, the Moon orbits Earth in 28 days. Because Earth orbits the Sun once a year, the Moon must also follow a path around the Sun. You might think that the Moon's path about the Sun is like the one shown in Figure 15. But the actual path of the Moon is quite different.

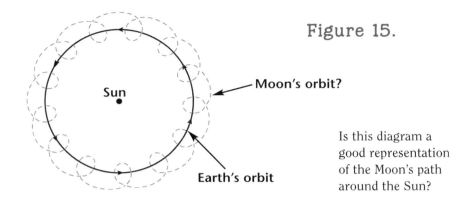

Figure 15.

Is this diagram a good representation of the Moon's path around the Sun?

Procedure:

1. To see what the Moon's orbit about the Sun looks like, you need to make a scale model. Earth is approximately 150,000,000 kilometers (93,000,000 mi) from the Sun. The distance between the Moon and Earth is approximately 400,000 kilometers (250,000 mi). The distances vary a little because the orbits are not perfect circles.

   You can make a scale model of part of the orbits of Earth and the Moon about the Sun. In this model, we will let one centimeter represent one million kilometers. Therefore, Earth's orbit will have a radius of 150 centimeters, or 1.5 meters (5 ft). To draw part of this orbit, you will need to tape together some large sheets of wrapping paper. The final sheet of paper should be a square about 1.6 meters (5 ft 3 in) on a side.

2. Let the lower left-hand corner of the paper represent the position of the Sun. Cut a piece of string a little longer than 1.5 meters (5 ft). Have a friend hold one end of the string on the lower left-hand corner of the paper. Hold a pencil or marking pen against the string at a point 150 centimeters (5 ft) from the end your friend is holding. Using the string as a radius, draw the representation of Earth's orbit as shown in Figure 16.

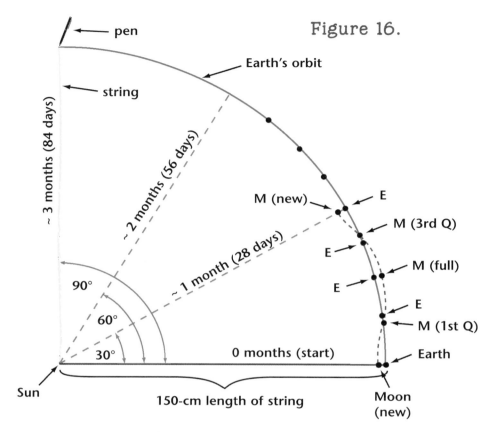

Figure 16.

Draw one quarter of Earth's orbit to a scale of 1 centimeter = 150,000,000 kilometers. Then draw the Moon's orbit about the Sun as a dotted line. The Moon on this scale will be 0.4 centimeters from Earth. The distance is somewhat exaggerated in this drawing.

3. Next, using a protractor and a meterstick, draw radii from the Sun to Earth at 0 degrees, 30 degrees, 60 degrees, and 90 degrees. Since Earth travels 360 degrees around the Sun in one year, it will travel about 30 degrees (360 ÷ 12) in one month. Start with Earth (E) on the starting radius at 0 degrees and the Moon at a new moon position, as shown. Since the Moon (M) is about 400,000 kilometers (250,000 mi) from Earth, it will be 0.4 centimeters (0.15 in) closer to the Sun than Earth. This distance is too small to show on the scale drawing in Figure 16, so the distances between Moon and Earth are larger than they should be.

4. Mark Earth's position at one-week intervals as shown. Remember that the Moon moves one quarter of the way around Earth every seven days. So, after seven days from the new moon, the Moon has traveled counterclockwise around Earth to the first quarter moon. The Moon will move to positions representing new moon (start), first quarter, full moon, third quarter, new moon, and so on.

5. Mark Earth's and Moon's position at weekly intervals for the three-month section of Earth's orbit you have drawn. Then connect the Moon's successive positions with a dotted line.

Results and Conclusions

You now have a good representation of one quarter of the Moon's orbit about the Sun. Does it look like the orbital path shown in Figure 15? What sort of path does the Moon follow?

 Science Project Ideas

- Knowing the distance between the Earth and the Moon, design and carry out an experiment to measure the diameter of the Moon.

- Knowing the distance between the Earth and the Sun, design and carry out an experiment to measure the diameter of the Sun. Remember: *Never look directly at the Sun.*

EXPERIMENT 2.4

An Eclipse of the Moon

Question:
What causes a lunar eclipse?

Hypothesis:
A scale model can show how Earth's shadow causes an eclipse.

Materials:
- scissors
- soda straw
- coin
- white file card
- frosted lightbulb, socket, and electrical outlet
- tape
- dark room
- Styrofoam or clay balls 5 centimeters (2 in) and 1.2–1.3 centimeters (0.5 in) in diameter
- stick 1.5 meters (5 ft) long
- 2 small finishing nails

Procedure:

1. Shadows vary in darkness. To see the difference in darkness, use scissors to make a small slit in the top of a soda straw. Insert a coin in the slit. The straw can serve as a handle.

2. Hold a white file card several feet from a glowing frosted lightbulb in an otherwise dark room. Bring the coin near the card so that you see its dark shadow (umbra) on the paper. Now slowly move the coin away from the card. You will see the dark umbra grow smaller, while a fuzzy lighter shadow, the penumbra, grows larger (Figure 17b). Earth's shadow also has an umbra and a penumbra (Figure 17a). Save the coin and straw for the next experiment.

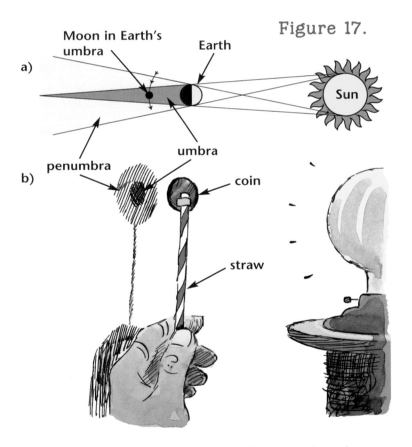

Figure 17.

a) Earth casts a shadow. When the Moon enters Earth's shadow, a lunar eclipse occurs.

b) A coin casts a shadow. The dark part of the shadow is the umbra. No light from the bulb reaches the umbra. The lighter part of the shadow is the penumbra. Some light reaches the penumbra.

Results and Conclusions

Occasionally, at the time of a full moon, Earth, Moon, and Sun lie along a line on the same plane, as shown in Figure 17a. Like any object in sunlight, Earth casts a shadow. We are in Earth's shadow every night after sunset. When the full moon enters that shadow, a lunar eclipse occurs.

Earth's shadow has an umbra and a penumbra. If you examine the drawing carefully, you can see that some light from the Sun reaches the penumbra. No direct sunlight reaches the umbra. The Moon darkens as it enters Earth's penumbra and becomes much darker if it reaches the umbra. The darkened Moon has a copper color, but it doesn't disappear. The atmosphere bends a little of the Sun's light around Earth so that some sunlight reaches the Moon. Therefore, our view of the Moon is never totally blocked by Earth's shadow, even when the Moon lies within the dark umbra of Earth's shadow.

Procedure:

1. You can make a scale model of a lunar eclipse. To do so you will need a Styrofoam or a clay ball 5 centimeters (2 in) in diameter and another with a diameter of 1.2–1.3 centimeters (0.5 in). You will also need a stick 1.5 meters (5 ft) long and two small finishing nails, one taped to each end of the stick, as shown in Figure 18. The large ball represents Earth. The small ball represents the Moon, which has a diameter that is a bit more than one-quarter Earth's diameter. The centers of Earth and Moon

are about 30 Earth-diameters apart. A stick 1.5 meters (5 ft) long will separate the model Earth and Moon by just about the distance needed for a scale model.

The real Sun can serve as the Sun in this model. It is much too far away to fit the scale. However, light rays reaching Earth from the Sun are almost parallel, so the Sun's size and distance aren't important for this model.

2. Hold the stick so that Earth is closest to the Sun, as shown in Figure 18. Tip and turn the stick until Sun, Earth, and Moon are in line. When they are, Earth's shadow will fall on the Moon. To see the Moon move into and out of Earth's shadow, turn the stick slightly on a horizontal plane, using Earth as the axis.

Figure 18.

Two spheres 1.5 meters (5 ft) apart can be used to make a scale model of Earth and the Moon. What conditions are needed to produce a lunar eclipse using this model?

Results and Conclusions

How much do you have to tilt the stick to move the Moon out of Earth's shadow? Why do you think an eclipse does not occur at the time of every full moon?

Save your model for the next experiment.

 Science Project Idea

Look closely at the shadow of a flagpole or a telephone pole. Notice that the shadow near the base of the pole is dark like an umbra. Farther out, the shadow shows a penumbra outside the umbra. If the shadow is long, its end may be fuzzy and light and have no umbra. How can you explain such a shadow? Does your shadow have a similar appearance?

EXPERIMENT 2.5

An Eclipse of the Sun

Question:
What causes a solar eclipse?

Hypothesis:
A model can show how the Moon's shadow causes an eclipse.

Materials:
- model you used in the previous experiment
- coin mounted on a soda straw used in the previous experiment
- frosted incandescent lightbulb and socket
- white file card or white wall

Procedure:

1. Turn the model you used in the previous experiment so that the Moon is closer than the Earth to the Sun. Move the stick until the Moon's shadow falls on Earth. You now have a model of a solar eclipse.

2. You can make another model of a solar eclipse that will show you what the Sun looks like during a total and a partial solar eclipse. An ordinary lighted frosted incandescent lightbulb can represent the Sun. Use the coin mounted on the soda straw that you used in the previous experiment to represent the Moon.

3. Stand several feet from the glowing lightbulb. Hold the coin in front of one eye and close your other eye. Move the coin back and forth until it covers all of the lightbulb. The entire bulb will disappear when the umbra of the coin's shadow falls on the pupil of your eye. The entire view of the bulb will be blocked from your eye. The coin (Moon) has totally eclipsed the bulb (Sun).

4. Move the coin slightly to the side. Part of the bulb becomes visible. Part of your eye is in the coin's umbra and part is in its penumbra. In the same way, the Moon, during a solar eclipse, casts a shadow on Earth. Where the shadow falls, it blocks from view part or all of the Sun. **Do not do this experiment outdoors using the real Sun!**

5. Move the coin closer to your eye. Does it block out more or less of the bulb? Slowly move the coin farther from your eye. Does the coin block out more or less of the bulb as you move it away? Hold the coin far enough away so that it blocks the center part of the lightbulb but leaves a ring of light around the edge. This is what happens during what is called an annular solar eclipse.

6. Replace your eye with a white file card or a white wall to represent Earth's surface. Let the coin's shadow fall on the card or the wall. You have an astronaut's view of Earth's surface during an eclipse. Can you find the region where there is a total eclipse? A partial eclipse? Can you move the coin so that no part of the umbra reaches the card or wall? What kind of an eclipse does this represent?

7. If you have an opportunity to view a solar eclipse, **never look at the Sun!** Even during an eclipse, the Sun is so bright it can severely damage your eyes. One way to view a solar eclipse is to make a pinhole image of the Sun. Make a pinhole in one side of a large cardboard box. Turn the box so that the pinhole faces the Sun. With your back to the Sun, place the box over your head. You can view the Sun's image on a sheet of white paper taped to the side of the box opposite the pinhole. Sunlight entering the box through the pinhole will form an image on the screen.

Look under a leafy tree during an eclipse. You will see many pinhole images of the eclipsed Sun.

Results and Conclusions

A solar eclipse occurs when the Moon's shadow falls on Earth. During a solar eclipse, the Sun, or part of it, is hidden by the Moon. Because the Moon is so small, its shadow covers only part of Earth. The Moon's shadow, like Earth's (and yours), has a dark portion (umbra) and a fuzzy portion (penumbra). As Figure 19a shows, the umbra touches only a tiny part of Earth's surface, if any. Only a small part of Earth will be covered by the darkest part of the Moon's shadow (the umbra), where all of the Sun's light is blocked by the Moon. As Earth, Sun, and Moon move, the Moon's umbra traces a narrow path across Earth's surface.

The width of this shadow never exceeds 274 kilometers (170 mi). Sometimes only the penumbra reaches Earth (see Figure 19b). When that happens, part of the Sun is always visible during the eclipse.

When you tried the model using a coin, the coin left a ring of light around the edge. This is what happens during an annular solar eclipse. In an annular eclipse, a thin ring of light is still visible all around the edge of the Sun because the umbra part of the Moon's shadow does not reach Earth's surface.

When the coin blocked out the top, bottom, or one side of the light-bulb, you had what happens during a partial eclipse, when you are in the penumbra portion of the Moon's shadow. Because the Moon's umbra never stretches more than 274 kilometers (170 mi) across Earth's surface, partial eclipses are more common than total eclipses.

 ## Science Project Ideas

- Use a pinhole image of the Sun and the known distance to the Sun (150,000,000 kilometers or 93,000,000 miles) to measure the Sun's diameter. Remember: *Never look directly at the Sun!*

- Mercury and Venus sometimes come between the Sun and the Earth. Why don't they cause eclipses of the Sun?

Figure 19.

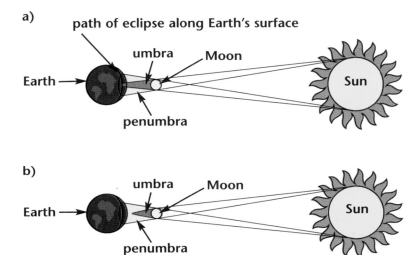

a)
path of eclipse along Earth's surface

b)

a) A solar eclipse occurs when the Moon's shadow falls on Earth. If the umbra reaches Earth's surface, people within the umbra will see a total solar eclipse. That is, the Sun will be completely blocked by the Moon. Within the penumbra, there will be a partial eclipse. Only part of the Sun will be blocked from view.

b) If the umbra does not reach Earth's surface, there will not be a total eclipse anywhere on Earth's surface.

CHAPTER 3

Our Changing Earth

Most of us think of Earth as one of the few unchanging things in our lives. But if we lived for centuries or millennia instead of years, we would see continents move and mountains rise or disappear. We also tend to think that water, which makes life on Earth possible, is found in oceans, lakes, and ponds. But there are huge amounts of water in aquifers under the ground we walk on. Wells are drilled to reach that water. Underground water is often the sole water source for entire communities.

◄In Iceland, the fracture between the American and European plates is visible. Over many years, such plates move and change the shape of Earth.

EXPERIMENT 3.1

Today's Continents and Yesterday's Pangaea

Question:

Were the continents once connected?

Hypothesis:

By arranging the shapes of the continents, you can see how they were once connected.

Materials:

- tracing paper
- globe or large map of the world
- pencil
- scissors
- construction paper

Geologists tell us that Earth's continents rest on plates about 80 to 160 kilometers (50 to 100 mi) thick. These plates are moving slowly as a result of forces beneath Earth's crust. About 200 million years ago, the continents were all together in a single landmass or continent called Pangaea. Since that time, movement of the plates has divided the continents and separated them by oceans and seas. Some remain connected by narrow strips of land.

Procedure:

1. To see how well the continents fit together, you can cut out the shape of each continent from construction paper. To do this, place a sheet of tracing paper over North America on a globe or large map of the world. Using a pencil, trace the outline of the continent on the paper. Use scissors to cut out the continent's shape. Then use the tracing paper as a template to cut the continent's shape from construction paper.

2. Repeat this process for each continent.

3. Now, arrange the paper continents so that they are next to one another. Can you make them fit together?

Results and Conclusions

If all the continents were once part of Pangaea, we might expect them to fit together like pieces of a jigsaw puzzle. Of course, the fits may not be perfect, because ocean levels have changed and continental edges have eroded over time.

Based on your observations, which continents do you think were the last to separate from one another? Which do you think were the first to separate? What makes you think so?

EXPERIMENT 3.2

Mountains and Plates

Question:

What caused the formation of mountains?

Hypothesis:

The movement of tectonic plates caused some mountains to form.

Materials:

- 2 pads of paper
- flat surface

Procedure:

1. To see how the collision of tectonic plates can give rise to mountains, you will need two pads of paper. Carefully push the pads together as shown in Figure 20.

2. What happened when you pushed the pads together? How did each pad move?

3. Push the pads together again. Did they move the same way?

4. Keep pushing the pads together to see how many different ways they can move.

Figure 20.

pads of paper

Mountains form when the plates covering Earth collide as they are moved by forces deep beneath Earth's surface. The paper pads represent two plates that are being pushed together.

Results and Conclusions

Earth's surface is constantly changing, but the changes are slow to occur. The mountains we see today arose when the plates on which continents rest collided.

When you pushed the pads of paper together, one of two things may have happened. In one case (a), the ends of both pads rise. In the other (b), one pad slides under the second, pushing it higher. In both cases, you can see how when plates collide, the land rises, forming mountains.

While continents slowly change position, their surfaces change as well because of erosion. Although erosion is generally a slow process, over millions of years it can wear away mountains. But erosion can also cause mountains to grow taller. Erosion makes the mountains lighter. This causes the mountains, which float on the denser mantle beneath the crust, to rise. In much the same way, a heavy cargo ship floats higher in the water when its cargo is removed.

 ## Science Project Ideas

- Design and build a seismograph that can detect earthquakes.

- Develop a model to show how the collision of tectonic plates can cause volcanic eruptions.

EXPERIMENT 3.3

Erosion by Water and Wind

Question:

How do water and wind cause erosion?

Hypothesis:

Water and wind slowly wear away at land formations, causing erosion.

Materials:

- **an adult**
- balance
- sink and faucet
- notebook and pencil
- 2 long, narrow cardboard boxes, such as candy boxes
- aluminum foil
- nail
- dry bar of soap
- clock or watch
- liquid measuring cup
- ruler
- soil
- grass seed
- water
- warm, well-lighted area
- books or blocks of wood
- plastic containers
- watering can
- 2 sheets of cardboard
- sand
- sandbox about 60 centimeters (2 ft) x 150 centimeters (5 ft)
- outdoor electrical outlet or extension cord
- glue
- wooden coffee stirrers or craft sticks
- fan, variable speed if available

Procedure:

1. Weigh a dry bar of soap. Record the weight and the time.

2. Put the soap in a sink and let a steady drip (not a stream) from a faucet fall on the center of the soap. Do this just before your family goes to bed so that water can drip on the soap all night.

3. The next morning, count the number of drops of water that are hitting the soap each minute. Record that number and the time. Then remove the bar of soap and let it dry.

4. When the soap is dry, reweigh it. How much soap eroded away? How many drops of water were required to produce the erosion? What is the rate of erosion in grams of soap per hour? What is the rate of erosion in grams of soap per liter of water? (It takes approximately 20,000 drops of water to fill a one-liter flask.)

Results and Conclusions

Erosion is not limited to mountains, but wherever it occurs, it is usually a slow process. Therefore, it is best to begin with an artificial example that will accelerate the process. The water eroded some of the soap just as it would a mountain or a coastline.

Procedure:

1. Line two long, narrow, cardboard boxes, such as candy boxes, with aluminum foil. Use a nail to punch holes in one end of each box, as shown in Figure 21a. Add equal amounts of soil to each box. Sprinkle grass seed over the soil in one box and gently work the seeds into the top of the soil. Sprinkle the soil in both boxes with water and keep the soil in both boxes moist. Place the boxes in a warm, well-lighted area.

2. When the grass is growing well, use books or blocks of wood to tilt both trays at the same angle, as shown in Figure 21b. Place a plastic container under the lower end of each box.

3. Using a watering can, sprinkle one liter (or 1 qt) of water over each box of soil. Eroded soil will collect in the containers. If very little erosion occurs, sprinkle another liter of water onto each box. Record the amount of erosion that occurred with each box.

4. Repeat the experiment, but this time fill both boxes with the same amount of loose, unseeded soil. Tilt one box so that its upper end is about twice as high as the other box's.

a)

box lined with aluminum foil

holes in end of box

b)

grass-covered soil   soil only

wood blocks or books

plastic containers to collect eroded soil

Figure 21.
a) Holes are made in one end of each box to allow eroded soil to exit.
b) Erosion from tilted boxes containing plain and grass-covered soil can be compared.

Results and Conclusions

In which soil, seeded or unseeded, was the erosion greater? Can you explain why? Would you expect more erosion on a grassy or a soil-covered slope?

When you increased the angle that the boxes were tilted at, in which box was there more erosion? Can you explain why? Would you expect more erosion to occur on steep mountains or on rolling hills that have a gentle slope? What is the effect of gravity on erosion?

Can you find evidence of soil erosion near your home? If you can, what might be done to reduce the erosion?

Procedure:

1. To see how wind can cause erosion, place two sheets of cardboard on level ground outdoors. Place a small pile of sand on each sheet. Sprinkle water on one pile until the sand is wet. Next, blow across both piles of sand. What do you observe? Explain how a severe drought can contribute to soil erosion.

2. To see how fences trap sand particles, you will need an outdoor sandbox. The box should be about 60 centimeters (2 ft) × 150 centimeters (5 ft) and contain dry sand about 5 centimeters (2 in) deep.

3. Place the box near an outdoor electrical outlet or **have an adult** connect an extension cord to an indoor outlet.

4. Make a miniature fence by gluing together wooden coffee stirrers or craft sticks as shown in Figure 22a. Leave about 5 centimeters (2 in) between the centers of the vertical sticks. Bury the lower end of the fence near one end of the box.

5. At the other end, use a fan to blow sand against the fence (see Figure 22b). **Stay behind the fan so that sand does not blow into your eyes**. Turn on the fan for about 30 seconds. Turn off the fan and look for any evidence of sand accumulating near the fence. Repeat the process several times, if necessary, until you see evidence of sand buildup around the fence. Where do sand dunes form?

Figure 22.

a) A model snow fence made by gluing together coffee stirrers or craft sticks.
b) An experiment to test the effect of fences on wind erosion.

6. Next, add more slats to the fence so that the sticks or stirrers are only about half as far apart. How does reducing the distance between the slats affect the buildup of sand?

Results and Conclusions

Sand particles and snowflakes can be carried long distances by wind. You may have seen snow fences along highways and similar fences on ocean beaches. The fences are designed to reduce the wind's speed, causing wind-borne particles to fall. In this way, snow is kept off roads and sand is prevented from blowing off beaches onto nearby land or highways.

How effective was your model at reducing erosion by wind? What would happen if a solid fence was used?

If your fan has variable speeds, you can investigate the effect of wind velocity on the fence's ability to accumulate sand.

How could you improve this model? Will two fences, one behind the other, work better than a single fence? How about V-shaped fences?

Science Project Ideas

- Design and conduct an experiment to find out how the erosion of soap is affected by the speed at which the water drops strike the soap.

- Design and conduct an experiment to find out how the erosion of sand and clay soils compare.

- Demonstrate how many farmers reduce the erosion of soil from their fields.

- Find out how severe drought caused the erosion of farmland in the United States during the 1930s.

EXPERIMENT 3.4

Glacial Erosion and Melting

Question:

How does a glacier erode the earth that it moves over?

Hypothesis:

Glaciers erode the earth by their movement and melting.

Materials:

- ice cubes
- sand
- bar of soap
- tray
- paper towel
- sunny window
- aluminum foil
- dry soil
- ground black pepper
- rubber bands
- dry leaves
- black and white construction paper
- natural winter ice
- lampblack, powdered charcoal, bone black charcoal, or pencil lead (graphite)
- 2 identical thermometers (-10°C–100°C)

Procedure:

1. Place an ice cube on some sand and allow it to stick to the bottom of the ice. You now have a miniature glacier. Then rub the sandy side of

the ice cube over a bar of soap to represent the earth. What does the sand under the ice do to the soap? What would an advancing glacier do to the earth below it?

2. Again, place the ice cube on the sand. This time, let the ice cube rest on the soap and melt, like a receding glacier. What is left after the ice melts? You have created a miniature moraine. A moraine is a deposit formed when glaciers melt, leaving the rocks and dirt that they carried in new places.

3. Place several identical ice cubes on a tray lined with a paper towel. Put the tray near a window where sunlight will fall on the ice cubes.

4. Cover each ice cube with a different material. You might use aluminum foil, dry soil, black pepper, and bits of dry leaves. If you have powdered carbon (lampblack, powdered charcoal, or bone black), use one or more of them. If you do not have any carbon, you can make some by scraping a piece of charcoal or the end of a pencil that has thick, black lead (graphite). One ice cube should be left uncovered to serve as a control. Which ice cube melts fastest?

5. To see why some ice cubes melted faster than others, you will need two identical thermometers. Wrap the bulb end of one thermometer with black construction paper. Wrap the second thermometer with white construction paper. Rubber bands can be used to hold the paper in place, as shown in Figure 23.

6. Set both thermometers side by side in sunlight. After 15 minutes, compare the temperatures. What do you find? How does the color of the paper affect its ability to absorb solar energy?

7. Sprinkle one area of a patch of natural winter ice with powdered charcoal or dark soil. How do you think the darkened area of ice will compare with the surrounding ice after several hours in the Sun? Was your prediction correct?

black paper   white paper

Figure 23.

Does color affect the absorption of solar energy?

Results and Conclusions

Twenty thousand years ago, a glacier, a layer of ice hundreds of feet thick, covered much of North America. Under its own weight, the glacier advanced, carving the earth beneath its surface. Glaciers transform the earth by their movement and melting.

Although much less extensive than during the ice ages, glaciers still exist. During droughts, airplanes are sometimes used to spray lampblack (powdered carbon) over a glacier. Why do you think they do this?

ⓌEXPERIMENT 3.5

Sun, Sand, Soil, and Water

Question:

How does Earth maintain moderate temperatures?

Hypothesis:

Water helps keep Earth cool.

Materials:

- **an adult**
- 3 identical aluminum cans
- balance for weighing
- garden soil
- water
- sand
- sunny place
- 3 thermometers (-10°C–110°C)
- sheet of cardboard
- black cloth
- clock or watch
- oven
- oven mitts
- hot pads

Procedure:

1. You will need to establish conditions that will cause different substances to receive the same amount of light and, therefore, the same amount of heat. To do this, obtain three empty identical aluminum cans. Place one can on a balance and add 200 grams (7 oz) of garden soil to the can. Pour an equal weight of water into a second can, and an equal weight of sand into a third can. Put a thermometer in each can. If their temperatures are not very nearly the same, leave them in a room until they are.

2. Record the temperature in each can. Then put the cans on a sheet of cardboard in a sunny place. Next, cover the cans evenly with a black cloth so that light falling onto the cloth will warm all the cans.

3. Record the temperature in each can at 15-minute intervals for at least two hours.

4. Next, remove the thermometer and have **an adult** place the cans in a warm oven (120°F, 49°C).

5. When soil, sand, and water are all at the same temperature, use oven mitts to remove all the cans and place them on hot pads in a cool place out of the sunlight. Which material warms fastest?

6. Again, record the temperature in each container at 15-minute intervals for two hours. Predict the substance—water, soil, or sand—that will cool slowest. Was your prediction correct?

Results and Conclusions

Earth's surface is covered with water and solid matter, such as rocks, soil, and plants. Were it not for the vast amounts of water on Earth, the planet would be too hot to support life. In this experiment, you saw that water keeps Earth at moderate temperatures.

Which substance—sand, garden soil, or water—shows the greatest capacity for absorbing heat; that is, which substance requires the greatest amount of heat to raise its temperature one degree? Which substance cooled the slowest? Why do you think one substance cools more slowly than the others? How does water help to keep Earth's temperature at a moderate level?

 # Science Project Ideas

- If possible, spend a warm day at a beach by the ocean or a large lake. By midday, you will probably notice that there is an onshore breeze—a wind that blows from the water toward the land. Explain the cause of the onshore breeze. Early the next morning, there will probably be an offshore breeze. Why?

- Look at Table 1 on page 104. Explain why the average summer and winter temperatures of cities near an ocean differ so much less than those of cities located inland, even though they may receive about the same amount of sunshine.

Table 1.
Average Summer and Winter Temperatures in Six U.S. Cities

City	Average January Temperature (°F)	Percent of Possible January Sunshine	Average July Temperature (°F)	Percent of Possible July Sunshine
San Francisco, CA	50.7	56	61.8	66
St. Louis, MO	28.8	52	78.9	69
Portland, ME	21.5	56	68.1	63
Fargo, ND	04.3	50	70.6	72
Seattle, WA	40.6	25	65.3	65
Spokane, WA	27.0	30	69.0	70

EXPERIMENT 3.6

Aquifers: Water Beneath the Ground

Question:

How can a pond be formed from an aquifer?

Hypothesis:

Since water collects in underground aquifers, digging into soil and reaching the aquifer can form a pond.

Materials:

- clay
- fine gravel or sand
- food coloring
- water
- aquarium, plastic shoe box, or large glass bowl
- watering can

Procedure:

1. You can make a model aquifer. To do so you will need clay, fine gravel or sand, and an aquarium, clear plastic shoe box, or large clear bowl.

2. First, cover the bottom of the clear vessel with a somewhat irregular layer of clay. The clay represents an impermeable layer of bedrock beneath the soil. Then add a layer of sand. Use the sand to form model hills, valleys, and deep wells. The shallowest sand should have a depth of at least one centimeter (0.4 in) above the "bedrock."

3. Use a watering can to sprinkle colored water onto the sand. Stop frequently to observe how the water seeps into the soil. Where the soil and underlying clay meet, the clear wall should provide a good cross-sectional view of the soil.

4. Observe the formation of the water table. As more water is added and the water table rises, observe the formation of "ponds." To see how these might dry up during a drought, watch what happens if no water is added for several days. Then add more water and notice the rising level of the "aquifer."

5. Use your model to show how a pond can be created by digging into soil.

Results and Conclusions

When rain falls to the ground, some of it evaporates quickly into the atmosphere. Some rain also runs off into streams and rivers that flow into ponds, lakes, and oceans. Some is absorbed by plants. The rest seeps into the ground, collecting as groundwater—the source of spring and well water.

Under the action of gravity, groundwater permeates (soaks) downward through the soil until it reaches a level of saturation; that is, until water fills all the spaces between soil and rock particles. The level dividing saturated from unsaturated soil is called the water table. The water table is the upper level of an aquifer. An aquifer is soil or rocks that can store large amounts of water between their particles. Sometimes the water table is higher than the ground, creating a pond, a lake, or a swamp.

 ## Science Project Ideas

- Aquifers are sometimes stacked like plates, one above the other. Can you build a model that has two aquifers, one above the other?

- What is an artesian well? Can you create a model of such a well?

- What might cause water to move in an aquifer? How can you use your model to illustrate such movement?

EXPERIMENT 3.7

Reaching the Aquifer: Permeability

Question:

Does the type of soil affect water's ability to reach an aquifer?

Hypothesis:

Some soils are more permeable than others, allowing water to easily seep into an aquifer.

Materials:

- nail
- 4 paper cups
- sand, gravel, clay, and garden soil
- measuring cup
- wooden coffee stirrers or small sticks
- 4 clear plastic or glass jars
- water

Procedure:

1. Use a nail to punch a hole in the bottom of four paper cups. Fill the cups about two thirds of the way with different soils. Put sand in one, gravel in another, clay in a third, and garden soil in a fourth.

2. Support the cups on wooden coffee stirrers or small sticks above clear plastic or glass jars, as shown in Figure 24.

3. Pour half a cup of water onto each type of soil. Allow the water to seep into the soil. What do you observe? What can you conclude about each soil's permeability?

Figure 24.

These drawings show an experiment to test soils for permeability.

paper
cup

sticks or
stirrers

clear
container

Results and Conclusions

For rain water to reach the aquifer, it must permeate (soak through) the soil above the water table. How rapidly it does this depends on the soil's permeability.

In this experiment, you tested the permeability of different soils. Through which soil does the water move fastest? Which type of soil retains the most water? How might soil type affect an aquifer?

You may have noticed gas bubbles as you watched the water seep into the soils. What do you think the gas is, and where do you think it came from?

EXPERIMENT 3.8

Ocean Water: Earth's Biggest Cover

Question:

How does seawater compare with fresh water?

Hypothesis:

Seawater and fresh water differ in taste, density, and conductivity.

Materials:

- tap water
- seawater from an ocean or kosher salt mixed with water
- 100-mL graduated cylinder
- balance for weighing
- 2 clear plastic vials
- food coloring
- eyedropper
- paper clips
- 3 insulated wires with alligator clips
- 6-volt dry-cell battery
- flashlight bulb

Procedure:

1. If you live near an ocean, collect some seawater and bring it home. If you do not live near an ocean, you can make some seawater. Add about 3.5 grams (one teaspoon) of kosher salt to 100 milliliters (34 oz) of water and stir until the salt dissolves.

2. To see how seawater differs from the water we drink, first place a drop of tap water and then a drop of seawater on your tongue. How do they differ in taste? **Do not drink more than a drop**.

3. Does seawater differ from drinking water in density? Density is defined as the mass or weight of a substance divided by its volume. One way to compare the densities of two substances is to weigh equal volumes of the two. You could do this by weighing 100 milliliters (34 oz) of tap water and then 100 milliliters (34 oz) of seawater. How do their densities compare?

4. You can also see how the densities differ using the method you used in Experiment 1.2. Fill one clear vial with tap water. Fill the other with seawater. Add one or two drops of food coloring to the seawater so that you can identify it. Use an eyedropper to remove some of the colored seawater from its vial. Place the end of the eyedropper below the surface of the clear tap water in the other vial. Slowly squeeze the bulb of the eyedropper so that a small amount of colored seawater enters the tap water. What happens to the seawater? Does it sink or float in the tap water? What does this tell you about the density of seawater as compared with drinking water?

   Can you make two distinct liquid layers, a colored and a clear, in the vial?

5. Next, repeat the experiment, but this time add food coloring to the tap water. What happens when you carefully squeeze a drop of colored tap water into the middle of the vial of clear seawater? Does it rise or sink? Does the result confirm what you observed before about the comparative density of tap water and seawater?

6. Some substances, such as copper, are good conductors of electricity. Other substances, such as glass, are not. To test tap water and sea-water for electrical conductivity, fill a clear vial with tap water. Slide two paper clips over the edge of the vial as shown in Figure 25. Half of each paper clip should be inside the vial.

7. Use three insulated wires with alligator clips to connect the paper clips to a 6-volt dry-cell battery and a flashlight bulb (see Figure 25). Does the bulb light?

8. Empty the vial and fill it with seawater. Then repeat the experiment. Does seawater conduct electricity? How can you tell?

Figure 25.

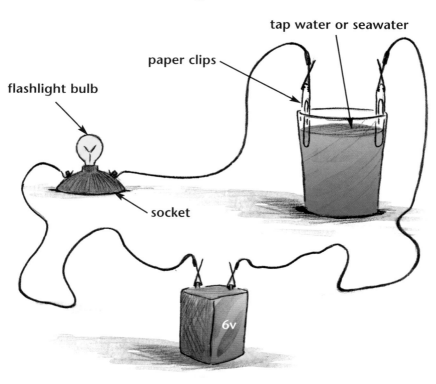

Will tap water conduct electricity? Will seawater?

Results and Conclusions

More than two thirds of Earth's surface is covered by ocean water, with depths as great as 11,000 meters (36,000 ft). Earth's abundance of water is believed to have come from several sources. These sources include rocks that came together as Earth formed, icy comets and meteorites that collided with Earth, and the rocks in Earth's mantle that are constantly emerging through the bottom of the oceans.

Ocean water differs from the water found in lakes and ponds because it contains salts. The primary salt dissolved in seawater is sodium chloride, the same salt you put on food. The concentration of salt in seawater is 3.5 percent.

The salt found in seawater makes it different from fresh water. As you saw in your experiments, seawater and fresh water differ in taste, density, and conductivity. Why are these differences important?

 ## Science Project Idea

Design and carry out an experiment that will allow you to separate the dissolved salts in seawater from the water. What practical use would this process have?

CHAPTER 4

Keeping Earth Healthy

E arth is the only planet we know to have living organisms. Life on Earth is possible because its air contains the oxygen we breathe, and its soil and oceans contain the water we drink. Of course, we can't drink seawater, but most of the water in rain comes from water that evaporated from the oceans. To preserve the air we breathe and the water we drink, we must avoid polluting them with harmful substances. Unless we do, Earth will become unhealthy for life. Some parts of it already are!

Since Earth's resources are limited, it makes sense to use things again and again rather than throwing them away. This process, known as recycling, is required in many communities.

◀By recycling waste and caring for plants, we can help keep Earth healthy.

EXPERIMENT 4.1

Sand as a Filter for Aquifers

Question:
Can sand act as a filter to remove particles and chemicals that may be washed into it?

Hypothesis:
Sand can act as a water filter.

Materials:
- nail
- 2 Styrofoam cups
- coffee filter
- 100-mL graduated cylinder
- clean sand
- marking pen
- 2 clear jars
- wooden coffee stirrers or craft sticks
- muddy water
- cold liquid coffee

Procedure:

1. Use a nail to punch a hole in the center of the bottom of two Styrofoam cups. Place a piece of a coffee filter over the holes in the bottoms of the cups. Then pour 100 mL (3.4 oz) of sand into each cup. (The filter will prevent the sand from leaking through the hole.)

2. Label one cup MUDDY WATER. Label the other cup COFFEE. Place each cup on a clear jar as shown in Figure 26. Use wooden coffee stirrers or craft sticks to support the cups.

3. Pour muddy water into the appropriate cup until the cup is full. Pour cold liquid coffee into the other cup until the cup is full.

4. Examine the liquid that drains out the bottom of both cups.

Figure 26.

Will sand remove small particles, such as mud, from water? Will it remove a chemical, such as coffee?

Results and Conclusions

Does the sand remove the mud particles from the muddy water? Does it remove the color from coffee? How can you check to be sure it was the sand that did the filtering and not the coffee filter?

Sand acts as a filter to remove solid contaminants from water that percolates through the ground into an aquifer. (Other soils will serve as filters as well.) However, soil does not filter out chemicals that dissolve in the groundwater or percolate through it.

 Science Project Ideas

- Design and carry out experiments to determine whether or not the size of soil particles affects their ability to filter particles that enter the soil. For instance, is fine sand a better filter than gravel?

- Design and carry out experiments to determine whether or not the size of soil particles affects the amount of water needed to saturate the soil.

- Design and carry out experiments to determine whether or not the size of soil particles affects the amount of water that the soil can retain.

EXPERIMENT 4.2

Model of a Polluted Aquifer

Question:

How can chemicals be removed from an aquifer?

Hypothesis:

Polluted water can be pumped out of an aquifer, filtered, and diluted with clean water.

Materials:

- sink or outdoor area
- clean, dry gravel
- clear plastic vial
- long eyedropper
- water
- scissors
- large-diameter drinking straw or 2 regular drinking straws and tape
- pencil
- food coloring

Procedure:

1. Do this experiment outdoors or in a sink. Add clean, dry gravel to a clear plastic vial until it is about three-fourths full. The gravel represents the ground in your model.

2. Next, fill an eyedropper with water. Use the eyedropper to "rain" on the ground in the vial. Watch the water percolate between the soil particles as you continue to add rain to the ground. Continue adding rain until the ground is saturated and a pond forms above the gravel.

3. Using scissors, cut a drinking straw with a large diameter so that its length is the same as the height of the vial. If you can't find a straw with a large diameter, cut two ordinary straws in the same way, then cut them lengthwise and tape them together to make a straw with a bigger diameter. The straw's diameter needs to be large enough to allow the eyedropper to fit into it.

4. Use a pencil to "drill" a well. Then use the straw to make a casing for the well as shown in Figure 27. The eyedropper can be used to pump water from your miniature aquifer. What happens to the pond as water is pumped out of the aquifer? Can you explain what happened to the pond?

Figure 27.

This model of an aquifer uses gravel to represent the ground, a straw to represent a well drilled into the aquifer, and an eyedropper to pump water from the aquifer through the well. One or two drops of food coloring can represent a pollutant, such as a gasoline spill.

"pump"

"well"

"pond"

5. Use one or two drops of food coloring to add a "pollutant" to the ground at a point away from the well. (The food coloring might represent a gasoline spill that has contaminated the soil.)

6. Add more rain to the ground. What happens to the pollution as rain enters the aquifer? Now pump more water from the aquifer. Do you see the pollutant moving toward the well?

7. Continue to add rain and pump water from the aquifer. Can you detect pollution in the well water?

Results and Conclusions

Soil does not filter out chemical pollutants. Chemicals in the soil may be spread when water enters the soil. As more water enters the soil, however, the concentration of the chemicals is diluted.

One way to clean up a polluted aquifer is to repeatedly pump water from the aquifer, filter it, and return it to the aquifer. Rain and filtered water will gradually dilute the pollution until the water is again safe to drink. Without filtering, how many pumpings and "rainstorms" are required to clean up your model aquifer?

EXPERIMENT 4.3

Some Do, Some Don't:
The Decomposition Story

Question:
What substances will decompose?

Hypothesis:
Organic matter from plants or animals
will decompose.

Materials:
- food waste, such as
  lettuce leaves,
  apple cores,
  or potato peels
- yard waste, such as
  grass clippings,
  shredded weeds,
  or leaves
- soil
- metal, such as
  aluminum foil
- synthetic cloth,
  such as nylon
- small spade
- water

- cloth from natural
  sources, such as
  cotton or wool
- plastic bag or pieces of
  Styrofoam
- recycled paper and
  new paper
- coffee stirrers
  or craft sticks
- waterproof pen
  or pencil
- ruler
- plastic containers, such
  as margarine tubs

Procedure:

1. Bury samples of different materials in warm, damp soil. Some materials you might try include (1) food waste, such as lettuce leaves, apple cores, or potato peels; (2) yard waste, such as grass clippings, shredded weeds, or leaves; (3) cloth from natural sources, such as cotton or wool, and synthetic cloth, such as nylon; (4) a plastic bag or pieces of Styrofoam; (5) metal, such as aluminum foil; and (6) paper, both recycled and new.

2. If you have a yard, use a small spade to dig a small hole about 10 centimeters (4 in) deep for each sample. Put the sample in the hole and cover it up with the dirt you removed. Push a coffee stirrer or craft stick into the center of the covered hole. The stick can be labeled with a waterproof pen or a pencil so that you can identify the buried material later when you dig it up. Do this for each sample. If the soil becomes dry, water it from time to time.

   If you do not have a yard, place the samples in plastic containers, such as margarine tubs. Label the containers, cover each sample with soil (not potting soil), and put them in a warm place. Keep the soil damp, not wet, by adding water occasionally.

3. After one month, dig up each sample. Which ones show evidence of decomposition? Which ones seem not to have decomposed at all?

4. Cover up the samples once more and check them again after another month or so. Continue to do this for as long as possible. Are there some substances that still show no signs of decomposition after many months in the soil?

Results and Conclusions

Some waste materials that we discard are biodegradable. Microorganisms in the soil decompose them, and they become part of Earth's soil and air. Other materials do not decompose and will remain for years in a landfill or as pollution. In this experiment, you saw that some materials degrade more quickly than others. Most substances will degrade if given enough time. Are there some substances that will never degrade?

EXPERIMENT 4.4

Don't Toss It! Compost It!

Question:

How can most food waste be reused?

Hypothesis:

Composting turns most food waste into rich soil for your garden.

Materials:

- **an adult**
- two or three 120-liter (32-gal) plastic trashcans
- bricks
- backyard
- drill
- pine needles or green twigs
- food wastes
- 3.5-liter (1-gal) plastic container with cover
- sink
- blender (optional)
- water
- grass clippings
- chopped leaves or straw
- elastic cord
- shovel or garden fork
- garden soil
- lumber
- wire
- ruler
- hooks and eyes
- kitchen waste, weeds, dead flowers, or vegetable leaves
- powdered limestone
- 6 hinges

Procedure:

1. Place a 120-liter (32-gal) plastic trashcan on four or five bricks in your backyard. The container should have 1-centimeter (⅜-in) holes about 5 centimeters (2 in) apart in its sides and bottom. **Ask an adult** to drill these holes for you. Cover the bottom of the container with pine needles or green twigs. This will allow air to reach the waste material that will be in the bottom of the container.

2. Collect food wastes, except for fatty materials, such as meat and bones, in a 3.5-liter (1-gal) covered, plastic container. Keep the container some-where out of the way, such as under the kitchen sink, so that the odor of old food will not bother anyone. You can collect fruit peels, carrot peels, potato peels, lettuce, and other plant waste from cooking. Do not include any matter that is not organic. Tear or cut the waste into small pieces before placing it in the container. You might even **ask an adult** to chop the material in a blender.

3. When the container is full, empty it into the large trash can you have prepared. Sprinkle a layer of pine needles, grass clippings, chopped leaves, or straw on the garbage each time you add waste to the large container. Then secure the cover to the container with an elastic cord.

4. While you are gradually filling the large container, prepare a second one just like the first. Again, **ask an adult** to drill the holes in the sides and bottom. Place the second large container beside the first one.

5. When the first container is full, use a shovel or a garden fork to transfer the waste from the first container into the second. The last waste added will then be on the bottom of the new container and the oldest waste on the top. Do not be alarmed to see insects or worms in the waste. They help to decompose and mix the waste.

6. Continue to fill the first container with new food waste. By the time you have filled the first container again, the waste in the second container may be ready for your garden or flower beds. If it is "done," it will be cool,

dark, and crumbly. It should have an earthy odor, not moldy or rotten. If it's not ready, transfer it to a third container identical to the first two. When it appears to be well decomposed, wheel it to your garden, dump it, and mix it with the garden soil.

7. Although it will take longer for complete decomposition, you can simply bury food wastes about 20 centimeters (8 in) below the surface of your garden. Dig up the buried waste after several months to see how rapidly it is rotting. Be sure to bury it again when you have finished inspecting it.

8. Another approach to composting is to build a container, such as the ones shown in Figure 28, to hold your compost. The wire allows air to reach the decaying matter. The hooks and eyes make it easy to move the compost pile because the fence can be taken apart and reassembled quickly. The larger size will cause the pile to heat up more quickly and increase the rate of decay. Add a cover to prevent animals from reaching the waste.

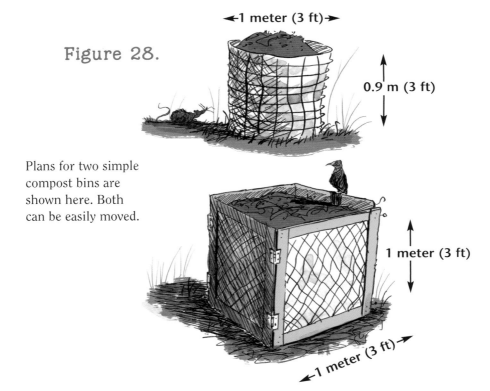

Figure 28.

◄1 meter (3 ft)➤

0.9 m (3 ft)

Plans for two simple compost bins are shown here. Both can be easily moved.

1 meter (3 ft)

◄1 meter (3 ft)➤

9. Start with a depth of about 15 centimeters (6 in) of organic material (kitchen waste, weeds, dead flowers, grass clippings, or vegetable leaves—no fats, meat, or bones). Add a 5-centimeter (2-in) layer of rich soil. Then sprinkle on a handful of powdered limestone before repeating the layering process with another layer of organic matter. You might also add wood ashes if you have a fireplace or charcoal ashes from a grill.

   If you have enough matter to build a pile 1 meter (3 ft) high, you may have useful soil within several months. If you build the compost pile more slowly, it will take longer—a year or more—to convert waste to garden soil. A compost pile that grows slowly doesn't develop enough heat to speed the growth and activity of the microorganisms that cause matter to decompose.

10. Add water, if necessary, to keep the compost damp but not wet. It should feel like a damp sponge from which water has been squeezed. It may be necessary to poke holes so that moisture and air can reach the inner parts of the pile.

11. When the original matter has changed in color and consistency, turn the pile over. This is easily done by unhooking the wire fence and moving it so that it is next to the pile. Then use a shovel or a garden fork to move the compost pile to its new location. The recently added matter will now be on the bottom of the pile and the original matter will be on top.

Results and Conclusions

Organic matter—matter that is or was living—will decompose, provided the bacteria and fungi normally found in soils are present. Some of the bacteria and fungi that decompose organic matter are anaerobic. They do not need oxygen to live, and they can digest plant and animal remains in the absence of air. In addition to moisture and warmth, "bugs" that cause decomposition need carbon as an energy source and nitrogen to make protein for their own cells. Plant matter, such as straw, leaves, and sawdust, can provide carbon. Grass clippings, humus, or green vegetables in garbage can provide the nitrogen.

Since the beginning of agriculture, farmers have spread manure on their soil, buried garbage in their gardens, and plowed green rye grass back into the ground. These materials then decompose, providing new soil and nourishment for plants. But you do not have to be a farmer to compost.

Composting is a way to increase the rate at which organic matter decomposes. Many landfills compost yard wastes and garbage to reduce the volume of material going into the landfill. The compost provides a rich soil that can be sold or given away for use in gardens and flower beds.

EXPERIMENT 4.5

Factors that Affect Composting

Question:

What composting techniques work best?

Hypothesis:

You can test different ways of composting by changing the materials you put together in miniature compost piles.

Materials:

- **an adult**
- 5 large plastic containers
- garden soil
- food wastes
- leaves
- water
- 10-5-10 fertilizer
- blender or food processor
- grass clippings
- earthworms
- thermometer (-10°C–110°C)
- small garden tool

Procedure:

1. Obtain five large plastic tubs, each can hold about 19 liters (5 gal).

2. Fill each tub with alternate layers of soil to a depth of 2.5 centimeters (1 in), organic waste to a depth of 5 centimeters (2 in), a sprinkling of 10-5-10 fertilizer, and enough water to dampen throughout. Repeat this layering until the tub is filled.

In one container, use food wastes (no fat, bones, or meat) as the organic layer. In a second, use chopped leaves as the organic layer. **Ask an adult** to use a blender or a food processor to chop the leaves into small pieces. In a third, use grass clippings for the organic layer. In a fourth, use food wastes again, but this time **ask an adult** to use a blender or a food processor to chop the food into small pieces. In a fifth, use chopped leaves as the organic material, and add a few earthworms to the container.

3. Keep all the tubs in a warm, dry place. Add water when necessary to keep the material as damp as a squeezed sponge.

4. Because these miniature compost piles are so small, their temperatures will not rise as high as those with a large volume. Nevertheless, you can use a thermometer to measure the temperature at the center of each miniature compost pile every day. Which tub gets warmest?

5. After the temperature in a tub reaches a peak and starts to fall, use a small garden tool to mix the compost. This will allow more air to reach the decaying material.

6. After all the miniature compost piles have turned to soil, they can be added to a garden.

Results and Conclusions

You should have seen different results based on the materials being composted. Which organic matter decays faster: food wastes, leaves, or grass clippings? How does chopping the matter into small pieces affect the rate of decay within the pile? What effect do earthworms have on the decay process?

EXPERIMENT 4.6

The Greenhouse Effect and Global Warming

Question:

How does the greenhouse effect influence temperature?

Hypothesis:

The greenhouse effect increases the air's temperature.

Materials:

- 2 identical thermometers
- clear plastic container that can be closed
- bright sunlight
- black paper
- automobile

Procedure:

1. Find two identical thermometers. Place one in a clear plastic container that can be closed. It will serve as the greenhouse. Put the box with the enclosed thermometer in bright sunlight. Place the second

thermometer beside the plastic box, as shown in Figure 29. Watch both thermometers for a few minutes. What do you conclude?

2. Predict what you think will happen if you line the box with black paper and repeat the experiment. Try it. Was your prediction correct?

3. Close the windows of a car that is at rest in sunlight. Half an hour later, return to the car. What do you notice as you enter the vehicle?

Figure 29.

How does the temperature inside this mini greenhouse compare with the temperature outside the greenhouse?

Results and Conclusions

Air is a mixture of gases. Twenty-one percent of air is oxygen, 78 percent is nitrogen, and almost one percent is argon. There are also small (trace) amounts of carbon dioxide, methane, nitrous oxide, ozone, and other gases, including water vapor. (The concentration of water vapor varies greatly and may be as high as one percent.) These trace gases, particularly carbon dioxide and water vapor, are called greenhouse gases.

About half the radiant energy (light, including infrared and ultraviolet) from the Sun reaches Earth's surface and warms it. The other half is reflected into space by the atmosphere. Of the half that warms Earth's surface, much of it would be radiated right back into space as infrared radiation were it not for the greenhouse gases. These gases, like the glass in a greenhouse, are transparent to short light waves (ultraviolet radiation) from the Sun. However, they absorb much of the longer-wave (infrared) energy released by Earth's surface. By preventing this energy from escaping into space, these gases create a warm blanket that covers Earth. Without these greenhouse gases, Earth would be colder, perhaps too cold to support life. On the other hand, if the concentration of greenhouse gases increases, Earth could become warmer.

Since 1880, the concentration of carbon dioxide in the atmosphere has increased from 290 ppm (parts per million) to 360 ppm, an increase of nearly 25 percent. During that same period of time, Earth's average temperature has increased by about 0.7°C, or 1.25°F. The increased levels of carbon dioxide in the atmosphere are causing Earth's average temperature to increase. Many scientists believe the increase in atmospheric carbon dioxide is making Earth warmer. This is called global warming.

CHAPTER 5

Mapping Earth

Maps are scaled drawings of part or all of Earth's surface. A map may show the boundaries of a person's property, a region of wilderness, or the entire world. Road maps, found in almost every car, are the most commonly used maps. They show a bird's-eye view of the relative locations and intersections of roads.

Many maps are based on photographs taken from airplanes. Landmarks on the photographs are matched with known points on the ground whose latitude and longitude are known. Using this data, the maps are drawn and labels are added.

The maps you will make are based on measurements and directions established from compass readings and a benchmark. Such techniques are still used to make maps of properties and to establish boundary lines.

◀ From left to right: a prism, total station, and GPS unit are set up in a field. The prism and total station are devices that are used to survey land and make maps. The GPS unit can be used to pinpoint the device's location.

EXPERIMENT 5.1

Mapping a Room

Question:

How do you make a map to scale?

Hypothesis:

Maps are made to scale by representing a
large length by a much smaller one.

Materials:

- bedroom or classroom
- tape measure
- sheet of paper,
  preferably
  graph paper
- ruler
- pencil
- protractor if graph
  paper is not available

Procedure:

1. Make a map of your bedroom or classroom. First, measure the length and width of the room.

2. Choose a scale that will allow you to fit the room's dimensions on a sheet of paper. For example, one centimeter on your paper might be used to represent 50 centimeters of the room's length and width. This would be a scale of 1:50. Or you might use one inch to represent one foot. This would be a 1:12 scale.

3. A protractor will help you to draw right angles. (If you have graph paper, it will make your task easier because the horizontal and vertical lines are at right angles.)

4. Once you have made the scale drawing of the room's dimensions, how can you add the furniture to your map?

Results and Conclusions

Maps are useful in determining how close one thing is to another. Maps must be made to scale in order to give an accurate representation of this.

EXPERIMENT 5.2

Maps, Magnets, and Earth's Magnetic Field

Question:

Why does a compass needle not point toward true north; that is, toward Earth's North Pole?

Hypothesis:

A compass needle points toward Earth's magnetic north.

Materials:

- clear night
- partner(s)
- stakes or sticks
- sunny day
- tape measure or ruler
- compass
- thread
- 2 bar magnets
- table far from any metal objects
- white paper
- pencil
- iron filings or steel wool and scissors
- tape
- thin cardboard

In making the map in the previous experiment you probably did not consider how the room was oriented with regard to geographical directions. Directions become very important when maps are made of roads, property boundaries, town and city lines, maps for hikers, and so on. In fact, almost any map will show the direction that is north as well as the map's scale (in/mi, cm/km, in/yd, etc.).

Here are two ways to find the direction we call true north.

Procedure:

1. On a clear night, find the North Star (Polaris; see Experiment 1.5). Because Polaris lies almost directly above Earth's North Pole, it can be used to find true north.

2. Establish a sight line to Polaris. Have a partner stand under that sight line. Then place two sticks in the ground, one where you are standing and one where your partner is standing. A line from your stake to hers points toward true north (see Figure 30a).

3. Another method to find true north can be done in the daytime. Place a stake in the ground. In the northern hemisphere, the stake's shadow will be shortest when the Sun is due south and at its highest point in the sky. Because the Sun is due south, its shadow will point toward true north. You might think that midday, when the Sun is due south, will occur at noon. But this is seldom the case. The best way to find true north is to wait until the Sun is approaching its highest point in the sky. (**Never look directly at the Sun. It can seriously damage your eyes.**) At that time, begin marking the end of the stake's shadow. Continue to mark it at five-minute intervals until you are certain the shadow is growing longer.

Figure 30.

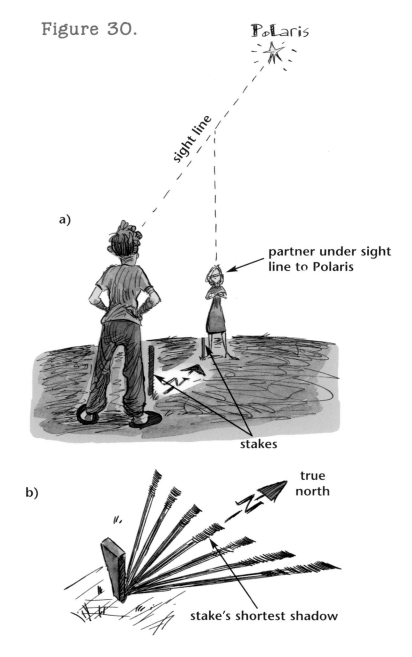

Finding true north using (a) the North Star (Polaris) and (b) the shortest shadow around midday.

4. Find the shortest shadow by measuring the distances from the stake to the marks you made at the ends of the shadows. A line from the stake to the end of the shortest shadow will point toward true north (see Figure 30b). Of course, in the southern hemisphere the shortest shadow will point toward true south.

5. Hold a good compass above the line that points toward true north. Unless you live along a line stretching from the panhandle of Florida to the western shore of Lake Superior, you will probably find that the compass needle is *not* parallel to the true-north line you have drawn. Why might this be?

6. Stand so that you are facing in the direction that the compass needle points. Hand the compass to a partner and ask her to stand several meters away from you. Ask your partner to also face in the direction that the compass needle points. If possible, repeat the process with a third person. You will find that all of you are facing in the same direction. In the same general location, the compass needle always points in the same direction.

7. Suspend a bar magnet from a thread. You will see it orient itself so that its north-seeking pole is north of its south-seeking pole. Next, hold one bar magnet close to a second. You will find that the north pole of one magnet attracts the south pole of the other. You will also find that the north poles of the two magnets repel one another, as do the south poles.

8. Put a bar magnet on a table far from any metal objects. Place a compass near the magnet's south-seeking (S) pole, as shown in Figure 31a. Notice that the north-seeking pole of the compass needle is attracted to (points toward) the south-seeking pole of the magnet.

Figure 31.

a) The north-seeking pole of a compass needle is attracted to the south-seeking pole of a bar magnet.

b) A compass can be used to map the magnetic field around a bar magnet.

c) The bar's magnetic field is revealed by mapping with a compass.

Results and Conclusions

As you probably know, a compass needle is a magnet that is free to turn. Every magnet has a north-seeking pole and a south-seeking pole. Sometimes the poles are marked with the letters N and S. The magnet of the compass is attracted to Earth's magnetic north pole.

The north-seeking poles of all magnets, including compass needles, point in a northerly direction when suspended above Earth's surface.

A compass needle's north-seeking pole will point in a particular direction when placed near a magnet. The direction is that of the magnetic field that surrounds the magnet. But the field has a strength as well as a direction. The strength is the force that the field can exert on another magnet or on moving electric charges.

Procedure:

1. You can map the magnetic field around a bar magnet. Place the magnet on a sheet of white paper. With a pencil, mark the direction that the north-seeking pole of the compass needle points as the compass is moved around the magnet (see Figure 31b). Begin with the compass near the north-seeking pole of the bar magnet. Simply move the compass in the direction the compass needle points to an adjacent position. Repeat this process until you reach the magnet's south-seeking pole.

2. If you repeat this a number of times, you can map the entire field around the magnet. However, you can map the field more easily using iron filings. These small pieces of iron behave as if they were tiny compass needles. You can probably borrow some iron filings from a science teacher or buy some at a hobby shop. Or you can make your own by using scissors to cut part of a roll of steel wool into tiny pieces over a sheet of paper. Use the paper to pour the particles into an empty spice shaker.

3. Once you have some iron filings, tape a sheet of white paper to a thin sheet of cardboard. Place the cardboard on a bar magnet. Then sprinkle some iron filings over the paper. Tap the cardboard gently. The filings will align themselves like tiny compass needles, revealing the field lines about the bar magnet (see Figure 31c).

Results and Conclusions

Earth's magnetic field looks much like the field you have just mapped. This would suggest that Earth acts as if it contained a huge bar magnet. Suppose you took a compass to Boothia Peninsula, north of Hudson Bay, about 1,900 kilometers (1,200 mi) from Earth's geographic North Pole. There, at about 76 degrees latitude, 100 degrees west longitude, you would find that the north-seeking pole of the compass needle points straight down. You would be standing over one of Earth's magnetic poles. Is the magnetic pole under Boothia Peninsula a north-seeking or a south-seeking pole? How would you know?

At a point in Antarctica near Dumont d'Urville, at about 67 degrees latitude, 140 degrees east longitude, you would be about 1,900 kilometers (1,200 mi) from Earth's South Pole. There you would find a compass needle's north-seeking pole points straight up. Is Earth's magnetic pole in Antarctica a north-seeking or a south-seeking pole? How would you know?

A compass needle seldom points toward true north. Earth's magnetic and geographic poles are about 1,900 kilometers (1,200 mi) apart. A compass near Boston, Massachusetts, will point about 15 degrees west of true north. A compass near San Diego, California, will point about 15 degrees east of true north. There is a line stretching from the Florida Panhandle to the western edge of Lake Superior along which a compass needle does point toward true north. Such a line is called an agonic line. The difference between true north and magnetic north as indicated by a compass is called the magnetic declination. However, Earth's magnetism is constantly changing. Therefore, charts showing the angles of magnetic declination on Earth's surface have to be revised frequently.

 ## Science Project Ideas

- Some scientists believe that birds and other animals use Earth's magnetic field to guide them as they migrate or move from place to place. What evidence can be offered to support this idea?

- If you lived south of the equator, how would you find true north?

EXPERIMENT 5.3

Mapping an Outdoor Area

Question:

How do you make a map of an outdoor area?

Hypothesis:

By using fixed points in an outdoor area, a map can be drawn.

Materials:

- thin piece of wood about 30 centimeters x 45 centimeters (12 in x 18 in)
- stick about 2.5 centimeters x 2.5 centimeters x 90 centimeters (1 in x 1 in x 35 in)
- 2 right-angle metal braces and screws
- large sheet of paper
- screwdriver
- cardboard
- sticks
- tape
- pencil
- magnetic compass
- straight pins
- ruler
- notebook
- partner
- tape measure
- lawn, ball field, school, or similar area

Procedure:

1. To map a large outdoor area, a mapping table is useful. You can make one from a thin piece of wood about 30 centimeters × 45 centimeters (12 in × 18 in), a stick about 2.5 centimeters × 2.5 centimeters × 90 centimeters (1 in × 1 in × 35 in), two right-angle metal braces, and screws (see Figure 32a).

2. A lawn, a ball field, or a school yard would make a reasonable area to map. Choose a point at one corner of the area as a place to start. Assume there is a benchmark at that point. A benchmark is a solid marker, such as a short concrete post for which the latitude and longitude have been established. You may actually be able to find one at the corner of a piece of property. If there is no benchmark, insert a stick to represent one at the corner you have chosen.

3. To map the area, you will make two sight lines to various objects from opposite ends of a baseline. Place the mapping table at the point you have chosen as a benchmark. It will serve as one end of the baseline. Cover the table with a sheet of cardboard and tape it in place. Then tape a large sheet of paper to the cardboard. Outline the position of the compass near one corner of the paper and leave it in place. On the paper, mark the direction of magnetic north according to the compass needle. Should the compass be moved, it can always be realigned from the mark and outline.

   Do you know the magnetic declination? If you do, mark the direction of true north on your map.

4. Use two pins to mark a sight line from a point near one corner of the paper to some identifiable object on the other side of the area you are mapping (see Figure 32b). Draw the sight line on the paper using a ruler and the pins. Repeat the process for a number of other objects within the area. Each time, check to be sure that the sight lines you drew earlier are still aligned properly. The object to which the sight line is directed can be identified by writing a number on the line. A record of the number and the object it identifies can be kept in a notebook.

5. Use your compass and sight lines to determine the direction of each object relative to magnetic north. For example, if the sight line is 15 degrees east of the direction indicated by the compass needle, its direction (bearing) is 15 degrees east of magnetic north. What is its direction relative to true north?

6. After you have drawn a number of sight lines to objects within the area you wish to map, ask a partner to stand at a point, say 30 meters (100 ft), toward another corner of the area to be mapped. Draw a sight line from your present position to the point where the person stands. Place a stake at the second position and move the mapping table there. The compass needle should point to the same mark you made earlier to indicate magnetic north.

7. Sight back along the sight line you just made to the mapping table's first position to be sure the mapping table is correctly oriented. The distance between these two positions constitutes the baseline you will use in preparing the map. The line between these two points on the paper corresponds to the two stakes in the ground. But, how far apart should those two points be on the paper?

Figure 32.

a)

45 cm

30 cm

90 cm

b)

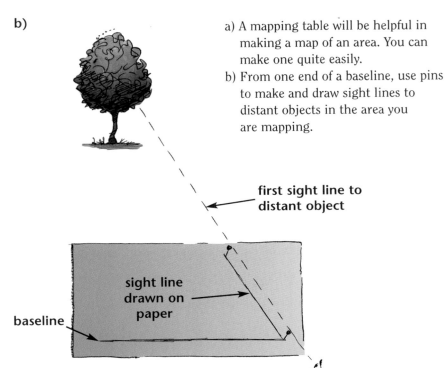

first sight line to
distant object

sight line
drawn on
paper

baseline

a) A mapping table will be helpful in
making a map of an area. You can
make one quite easily.

b) From one end of a baseline, use pins
to make and draw sight lines to
distant objects in the area you
are mapping.

8. The scale must be such that the map will fit on the paper. For example, suppose you choose to let one centimeter on the map equal one meter of ground (a scale of 1:100). If the ends of the baseline are 30 meters apart, set the second pin 30 centimeters from the first. Use that second pin and another to sight on the object that will require the greatest change in direction relative to the original sight line you drew to it from the bench-mark. For example, if you moved left to establish your baseline, sight on the object farthest to the right. Does the point you chose to represent the end of the baseline on the paper allow the new sight line to cross the older one? If it does, your scale will work. If it doesn't, shorten the baseline on the paper by choosing a scale with a greater ratio. For example, try letting 0.5 centimeters = 1.0 meter (a scale of 1:200).

9. Once you have a workable scale and the mapping table is properly positioned, draw new sight lines from this end of the baseline to each of the objects you sighted before. Be sure to check the table's orientation before and after you make each sight line.

Results and Conclusions

When you are finished, you will see that you have made a series of triangles. The base of each triangle is the same for all of them; it is the baseline on the paper. The sides of the triangles are the sight lines you drew to each object from opposite ends of the baseline. Each object on the map is at the apex of the individual triangles (see Figure 33). You might like to extend the baseline and make a third sight line to each object.

Figure 33.

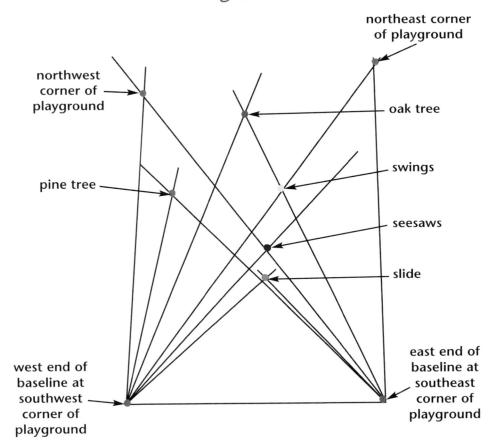

northeast corner
of playground

northwest
corner of
playground

oak tree

pine tree

swings

seesaws

slide

west end of
baseline at
southwest
corner of
playground

east end of
baseline at
southeast
corner of
playground

Sight lines drawn from the two ends of a baseline can be used
to map a playground.

Use the map and a ruler to predict the distances to each of the objects from each end of the baseline. Then measure the distances with a tape measure. How do the measured distances compare with your predictions based on the map? Finally, predict the distances between the objects using the map. Then measure the distances. How do the predicted and actual distances compare?

If your map is accurate, you can erase the sight lines and write the scale ratio on the map. You now have a map of the area.

 ## Science Project Ideas

- What is a contour map? Devise a model to show how contour maps are made.

- Make a contour map of a small area near your home.

Appendix
SCIENCE SUPPLY COMPANIES

Carolina Biological Supply Company
2700 York Road
Burlington, NC 27215-3398
(800) 334-5551
http://www.carolina.com

**Connecticut Valley Biological
Supply Company**
82 Valley Road
P.O. Box 326
Southampton, MA 01073
(800) 628-7748
http://www.ctvalleybio.com

Delta Education
80 Northwest Boulevard
P.O. Box 3000
Nashua, NH 03061-3000
(800) 258-1302
http://www.delta-education.com

Edmund Scientifics
60 Pearce Avenue
Tonawanda, NY 14150-6711
(800) 728-6999
http://scientificsonline.com

Educational Innovations, Inc.
362 Main Avenue
Norwalk, CT 06851
(888) 912-7474
http://www.teachersource.com

Fisher Science Education
4500 Turnberry Drive
Hanover Park, IL 60133
(800) 955-1177
http://www.fishersci.com

Frey Scientific
80 Northwest Boulevard
Nashua, NH 03063
(800) 225-3739
http://www.freyscientific.com/

NASCO-Fort Atkinson
901 Janesville Avenue
P.O. Box 901
Fort Atkinson, WI 53538-0901
(800) 558-9595
http://www.enasco.com/

NASCO-Modesto
4825 Stoddard Road
P.O. Box 3837
Modesto, CA 95352-3837
(800) 558-9595
http://www.enasco.com

Sargent-Welch
P.O. Box 4130
Buffalo, NY 14217
(800) 727-4368
http://www.sargentwelch.com

Science Kit & Boreal Laboratories
777 East Park Drive
P.O. Box 5003
Tonawanda, NY 14151-5003
(800) 828-7777
http://sciencekit.com

Ward's Natural Science
P.O. Box 92912
Rochester, NY 14692-9012
(800) 962-2660
http://www.wardsci.com

Further Reading

Bochinski, Julianne Blair. *The Complete Workbook for Science Fair Projects*. Hoboken, N.J.: Wiley, 2005.

Murrie, Steve. *Planet Earth: Guide to the Planet*. New York: Scholastic, 2009.

Oxlade, Chris. *Hands-on Science Projects: Earth: Find Out About the Planet, Volcanoes, Earthquakes and Weather with 50 Great Experiments and Projects, Over 300 Fantastic Photographs!* London: Southwater, 2009.

Vecchione, Glen. *Blue Ribbon Science Projects*. New York: Sterling Publishing Company, 2005.

Internet Addresses

The Exploratorium. Exploratorium Home Page.
 <http://www.exploratorium.edu>

Reeko's Mad Scientist Lab—Educational Experiments.
 <http://www.spartechsoftware.com/reeko>

Yahoo! Kids—Science.
 <http://kids.yahoo.com/science>

Index